HOW TO GIVE A SPEECH

HOW TO GIVE A SPEECH

REVISED EDITION
BY MARGARET RYAN

A SPEAK OUT, WRITE ON! BOOK
Franklin Watts
New York/Chicago/London/Toronto/Sydney

For Emily, again

Photographs copyright ©: Comstock, Inc.: pp. 8, 112 (both Sven Martson), 129 (Art Gingert); North Wind Picture Archives, Alfred, Me.: p. 23; Jay Mallin: pp. 25, 74, 83; Sygma/Ira Wyman: p. 31; Monkmeyer Press Photo/George Zimbel: p. 41; Photo Researchers/Rafael Macia: p. 48; Archive Photos, NYC: p. 56; UPI/Bettmann: p. 61; Reuters/Bettmann: pp. 69, 89, 102; Randy; Matusow: pp. 95, 119; The Bettmann Archive: p. 134.

Library of Congress Cataloging-in-Publication Data

Ryan, Margaret.
      How to give a speech / Margaret Ryan. — Rev. ed.
        p. cm.—(A speak out, write on! book)
      Includes bibliographical references (p.) and index.
      ISBN 0-531-11199-7 (lib. bdg.)—ISBN 0-531-15804-7 (pbk.)
        1. Public speaking—Juvenile literature.   [1. Public speaking.]
  I. Title.   II. Series.
PN4121.R913   1994
808.5'1—dc20   94-28074   CIP AC

CONTENTS

GIVE A SPEECH

So, you have to give a speech!

ONE

So, YOU HAVE TO GIVE A SPEECH!

The best impromptu speeches are the ones written well in advance.

—Ruth Gordon

Most people would rather die than give a speech. In fact, when a recent survey revealed what Americans fear most, death was fourth on the list; giving a speech was first.

Even veteran speechmakers suffer from fear of public speaking. The vice president of a $12 million corporation trembles visibly on his way to the podium each time he has to address a group—about once a week. Prominent authors, who have no trouble expressing their opinions on the page, sometimes struggle when it's time to take their ideas to the podium. As Susan Faludi, author of the best-selling and hard-hitting book *Backlash*, put it, "My fingers may belt out my views when I'm stationed before the computer, but stick a microphone in front of me and I'm a Victorian lady with the vapors." Anyone who has coached speakers can tell you there are only two kinds: those who let their fear stop them, and those who take their fear with them and put it to work.

Speechmaking is probably no mystery to you. Even if you haven't been asked to speak before, you've seen

9

and heard plenty of speeches: candidates for political office, the president of the United States on television, parents at town meetings, your classmates at assembly or commencement. Your school principal probably makes speeches all the time.

Giving and listening to speeches is a uniquely American entertainment. During the height of the 1992 U.S. presidential election campaign, a columnist in *The New Yorker* magazine called the political oration "a remarkably enduring form of American folk art." Speeches are one of the main forms of political discussion during election campaigns. Commentators make a living rating the speeches of those who run for office. And during the Democratic National Convention in New York City in 1992, even ordinary people were trading notes, as *The New Yorker* put it, "about the stolid earnest performance of Bill Bradley, the careful eloquence of Barbara Jordan, the banked-down fire of Jesse Jackson, and the twanging peroration of Governor Zell Miller."

Whether you're comfortable criticizing speeches or not, one thing about them is immediately obvious: some are more interesting than others. What makes the words of one speaker catch your imagination and linger in your memory, while others put you to sleep or slip your mind before you're out the door? Talent may separate the great from the competent, but talent alone does not make a great speech. Preparation makes performance possible. Good speakers know and practice the steps that lead to an interesting, effective speech.

Members of the audience don't see the preparation, of course; they see only its results. In this respect, speeches are like athletic events. You applaud and admire the triple jumps and spins of a figure skater, but unless you are a skater or a coach, the rigorous training, the repetition and practice that make the routine flawless remain invisible. The difference between a gold medalist and an also-ran includes talent, but all the talent in the world won't make up for a lack of preparation, persistence, and practice.

If you have any fear about giving a speech, and "I've never done it before" is part of the reason, take heart. Giving a speech is a skill, like driving a car, knitting a sweater, or playing a video game. It can be learned.

In fact, you already know plenty about giving a speech. It begins with your knowledge of yourself. Just as Barbara Jordan is eloquent, Jesse Jackson is fiery, and Bill Bradley is stolid, your speaking style will be an outgrowth of your personality. If you are witty and outgoing, you may succeed as a humorous, exuberant speaker. If you tend to be shy, perhaps more at home with books or computers or pets than on stage, you *may* become a tiger at the podium. But it's more likely that your style will be reserved and thoughtful.

There is room on the podium for the speaker of meticulous preparation and careful expression, for the emotional speaker whose stories of courage or compassion can move crowds to tears or to action, and for the witty speaker who makes us laugh. In fact, the most successful speakers are those who combine good humor, clear thinking, and emotional appeal—and who are comfortable being themselves in front of an audience.

As you prepare and give a speech, you may find some parts of the process easy. You might be great at thinking up topics, at researching, or at delivering your talk. Appreciate your strengths and build on them. Other tasks may be harder: perhaps organizing your thoughts, or modulating your voice, or thinking up attention-getting openings will be your challenge.

Maybe you need to find ways to introduce humor, quotations, or anecdotes into your speech. With practice, you can learn.

Learning to give a speech will help you fulfill school assignments. It will also give you a skill that will remain useful throughout your life. You will find the ability to express your thoughts important in your academic career, and in your professional development once school is behind you.

Those who aspire to a career in politics must, of course, learn the art of speaking. But sports stars, war heroes, and diplomats can have successful second careers as speakers, too. Today, even the most technically oriented business people are expected to make presentations and speeches. Good ideas are much more valuable when they're communicated persuasively to others.

There are other, less tangible rewards for learning how to prepare and give a speech: the excitement of having an audience really listening, and thinking about what you have to say; the satisfaction of expressing your thoughts clearly and persuasively.

There is even some pleasure to be gained from giving a speech: that corporate vice president who trembles on the way to the podium also cherishes the exhilaration once the speech is done.

Writing speeches can be an interesting career too for those who like research and writing but have no desire to stand before an audience. Politicians, business executives, and sports figures often need help drafting their remarks. And presidential speechwriters like Peggy Noonan and William Safire have shown that those who practice the so-called silent profession can go on to more outspoken careers of their own.

No matter how you feel about writing and giving a speech, learning how to prepare will make your job easier. This book outlines a step-by-step process used by business and professional speakers, by speakers who entertain, and by those who persuade and instruct. It can lead you toward a confident performance at the podium.

But this book can take you just so far. Only you can put this system for successful speaking to action; only you can prepare, practice, and perfect your own successful speaking style.

TWO

WHAT SHOULD YOU TALK ABOUT?

In Maine we have a saying that there's no point in speaking unless you can improve on silence.

—Edmund Muskie

Perhaps you are lucky enough to know what your topic is and what you want to say about it. Good for you! Go on to the next chapter. Begin to think about your audience, and start your research.

On the other hand, if you are having trouble choosing a topic, or struggling to bring an assigned topic down to a size and shape that are both manageable and compelling, read on.

A good speech entertains, instructs, informs, amuses, perhaps even amazes or impresses; it wins votes, hearts, a good grade, or an oratory contest. What you say may be original, it may be witty, it may be wise. But no matter what approach you take, you need a solid topic. And not just any topic, but one that interests you.

This is your chance to have your say, so take time to find and focus on a topic that fits your tastes, one you have some feeling for—or against. Love your topic or hate it, but if you are neutral your job will be hard. You can't expect your audience to care about what you are saying unless you care first. Boredom is highly contagious; audiences have little resistance to it.

Unfortunately, speakers aren't always permitted to select their own topics. Whether you are limited by an assignment ("Give a speech on the history of Poland") or told to talk about anything—but for no more than five minutes—you will be working with some restrictions. But you will also have some choice.

Consider all the ways topics come to you, and how you can work within each set of limitations and freedoms to find a subject that speaks to you, one you can speak about with confidence. You may be:

- Assigned a subject, or given a list of suggested topics and asked to choose.
- Speaking at an occasion that provides its own subject matter, such as a graduation (a look toward the future), a testimonial dinner (the good nature of the person being honored), an awards ceremony (the reason for the award), or a roast (a playful criticism of the guest of honor).
- Expected to speak with a specific purpose—to entertain, to inform, or to persuade—while the subject of your talk is left to you.
- Given a time limit, say, fifteen minutes, and allowed to speak on anything you like.

We'll consider each circumstance in turn.

ASSIGNED TOPICS

Whether it's one unavoidable assignment, such as the nuclear freeze, or a list of several topics from which you can choose, all assigned topics share a common flaw: they are too broad. Teachers usually assign broad topics by design; they want you to have room within the assignment to find an angle that interests you. And people who ask you to speak in nonschool situations may indicate a broad area they know will interest their audience, or one that will fit in with other topics on the program. But they rarely dictate the precise topic for your speech.

The most important thing to do with an assigned topic is to narrow it down to size. Let's take an example. Suppose you have been asked to make a speech about baseball and given a time limit of fifteen minutes. Obviously, you can't cover the entire subject in that little time. So you will have to whittle down the big topic to more sensible proportions.

Begin by considering your interests. You need an angle that appeals to you. Do you care about the history of the designated hitter? Or how television has changed the game? Are you interested in the women's baseball league that flourished during World War II? Or are you concerned about foreign companies owning American teams, or the weakened role of the commissioner of baseball? Maybe you are interested in the contribution Jackie Robinson made to the sport, or you'd like to talk about Shoeless Joe Jackson. Maybe baseball movies, or baseball cards, appeal to you.

If you're the business type, you might want to learn and talk about who owns the clubs, how they're financed, and how corporate ownership affects the sport. Maybe you've heard that baseball is a legal monopoly, and you'd like to know more—and tell all. You could be a fan concerned about the high price of tickets, or the tendency of teams to move from urban centers to the suburbs, or the design of new stadiums, such as Camden Yards in Baltimore. You could talk about Reggie Jackson's entry into the Hall of Fame. Or you could talk about your experience playing Little League—or not playing Little League—and what it meant to you.

A subject such as baseball contains an almost infinite number of fifteen-minute topics. Is one better than another? Yes. How do you know which one it is? It is the one that most interests you.

Now you have some idea of how to think about the subject of baseball. But what if you have trouble thinking up manageable topics within your subject area? One way is to ask yourself the kinds of questions reporters rely on: who, what, when, where, why, and how.

Suppose you have to speak on the federal budget deficit. You would ask yourself questions like these:

- Who was president when the deficit was largest? Smallest? When it grew the fastest? Who benefits when the deficit is large? Who suffers?
- What does the borrowed money buy? What does the deficit mean to your future? To your audience's future?
- Why do we have a budget deficit? Why do people worry about it?
- Have there been periods of no deficit? How has it changed over time? What forces affect the deficit?
- How is our nation's practice of borrowing different from those of other nations? How are various politicians and political parties suggesting that the deficit be reduced?

Remember to ask, "How do I feel about it?" If the whole idea of borrowing huge sums that future generations will have to repay makes you angry, you may have found the angle you need to turn a broad topic into a manageable one. It certainly worked for Ross Perot in the 1992 presidential campaign!

BRAINSTORMING

Try brainstorming if your topic doesn't generate any immediately exciting notions. It's easy and fun to do. Write your topic in the center of a sheet of paper, and then scribble around it all the ideas you can think of.

Don't be hard on your ideas. Just let yourself go—think them up and write them down. Be ridiculous. Be outrageous. Sometimes wild ideas lead to the best speeches.

If you find yourself staring at the topic and unable to come up with a single thought, try brainstorming with a friend or a group of friends.

The goal is to generate lots of ideas without attacking or judging them. All of you should be free with your thoughts. Even if they seem silly, blurt them out. But don't discuss them during the brainstorm, or criticize with even a look or a groan. One person should be the note taker, writing all the ideas down.

When you've emptied your heads of ideas and set them all down on paper, take a few minutes to read them over and think them through. Try to figure out why you thought of Cadillacs when the subject was baseball. Why did Bart Simpson come to mind when the topic was the budget deficit? Is the connection interesting? Does it lead you toward a workable topic?

Once you've thought about all the possible angles, select the three strongest ideas and consider them in more depth. Which one do you like best? Which would be easiest to research, in terms of both time and the resources available to you? Which would be hardest to talk about and why? Which would be the most fun for you? For your audience?

Next, take your time limit into account. Most speeches allow you to present only a single strong idea, along with supporting reasons, arguments, and information. For example, you probably won't be able to discuss both baseball in Japan and women in the major leagues in a single speech, unless you are talking about women in Japanese major-league baseball.

And one main point—supported by three ideas—is about all your audience will absorb, no matter how much you try to fit in. The "less is more" theory holds true in speechmaking: you can make one point superbly, two well, three weakly, and so on. Try to keep your topic straightforward and simple. Remember that a speech is not a dissertation. Your audience will be listening, not reading. You will need to make it easy for them to follow along, because they won't be able to go back and reread a sentence or a section that puzzles them.

FINDING AN ANGLE

Once you've got a topic, make sure you have an angle on it—a point of view. What is the main thing you want to say about women in baseball? Or about Little League? Or the national debt? Consider these topics and angles:

TOPIC	ANGLE
Women in baseball	Let women into the major leagues! Keep women out of baseball.
Japanese baseball	More American than our own Another game
Foreign ownership of teams	New life for an old sport Death of the American pastime

Any of the angles would make good manageable fifteen-minute speech material. How do you choose? Again, think about what interests you, how you feel about the subject.

What if none of the ideas grabs you? Give yourself some time. One topic may keep floating up into consciousness, nagging at you when you least expect it. If so, that's the one. If none of them grabs you, go back and brainstorm again if you have time.

If you don't have time—and let's face it, sometimes you won't—close your eyes, pick a topic, and go with it. Sometimes just doing the assignment is enough. Don't worry about it. You may find yourself caring more as you learn more about your topic. Your research may lead you to tweak your topic a little, to put a spin on it that makes it more intriguing. Just pick the topic you feel warmest toward and go for it.

SPEAKING TO AN OCCASION

Whether it's a graduation ceremony, a rally, a testimonial dinner or roast, or an awards banquet, certain speaking occasions come with their own ready-made subject matter.

Professional speechwriters are often asked to write what are known as occasional speeches—to be delivered at a special occasion. Their solution to the problem of "making it new" is to take advantage of every detail of the event. In other words, they focus on the specifics that make this graduation, or testimonial, or rally different from others.

For the dedication of the American Adventure Pavilion at Walt Disney's Epcot Center, for example, the speechwriter's challenge was to say, "We are glad to be sponsoring this building" in a way that engaged the audience. To breathe life into the topic, she took advantage of the date of the ceremony, Columbus Day, and began by referring to Christopher Columbus's trip and the assistance provided by Queen Isabella. Images of travel, travel services, and Columbus's voyage tied in neatly to the participation of American Express, with its travel services, in the sponsorship of a building called the American Adventure. It was enough to turn a dull subject into a brief, fresh speech.

Take a tip from the professionals. For an occasional speech, ask yourself:

- Is the date/season/time of year related to the event in any significant way? Did anything else happen on this date which can be related to the subject of my speech? Check an almanac; you may find yourself speaking on the day the *Titanic* sank, or the day humans first walked on the moon, or Sigmund Freud's birthday. See if you can use these facts in your introduction.
- What would people at the first event of this type think of this one? How was the first graduating class from your high school different from this one, for example? Perhaps only women attended your school in those days, or the class was very small, or included people who later became famous.
- How would this occasion look to people in the future—ten, twenty, or fifty years from now?
- How would this event look to a figure in history? A creature from another planet? A movie star? Someone from another country or culture?

Finding a fresh perspective is key. But remember, you must tie whatever interesting facts you turn up into the event at hand. The facts must be relevant to your audience, your event.

SPEECHES WITH A PURPOSE

Suppose you've been told to give a speech with a specific purpose—to inform, say, or to persuade—and the topic of the speech is left entirely to you.

The Gettysburg Address

Perhaps the most famous occasional speech ever written is Abraham Lincoln's Gettysburg Address. The occasion: the dedication of a cemetery on the site of a famous and bloody Civil War battle.

In *Lincoln at Gettysburg*, Garry Wills tells the story of this famous speech. What's remarkable about it?

First, in a few sentences, Lincoln redefined the aims of the Civil War. It was not just about keeping the Union intact; it was about freedom and equality for all Americans. Lincoln asserted that our nation was "dedicated to the proposition that all men are created equal," which could not be true while slavery was legal.

Second, Lincoln accomplished a revolution in style. The text is shorter, simpler, and clearer than most speeches of that day. Before the Gettysburg Address, complex sentences and complicated language were common in speeches. Lincoln used ordinary language, short sentences, and a concise style. He used few words, but said as much as possible in them.

At Gettysburg, Lincoln set a standard for American political rhetoric that remains until this day.

Abraham Lincoln delivering the Gettysburg Address— a model of an "occasional" speech.

Of course, you know to pick a topic that interests you; it's no good trying to inform an audience about stamp collecting if the sight of stamps bores you stiff. Similarly, you can't persuade your listeners to care about the current state of the budget deficit if thinking about it makes you yawn.

Begin with your interests. List the three things you currently care about most. How much do you know about each? Can you speak from close or personal experience on the difficulty of breaking into the music business? Could you instruct an audience on ways to create computer graphics? Or are robots and their uses your special concerns? Maybe you've been studying the English flower garden in preparation for spring planting, and you now know more about Gertrude Jekyll's color schemes than anyone else in town. Chances are you have some special interest you can share.

This is probably not the time to unravel the intricacies of unified field theory. Unless you already have a solid grounding in astrophysics, you probably won't have time to get the facts down yourself, let alone develop a perspective that would make for an interesting speech.

And don't worry if the things you know about—baseball, robots, how to give a perfect manicure, or how to groom a horse—don't sound as impressive as the time-space continuum. Your audience will probably prefer learning something useful that you really know about to being lectured on concepts even you have trouble understanding.

If you've been asked to persuade, you'll need to take a position you believe in—or at least, one that you feel is defensible. Though it is sometimes interesting to argue the opposite point of view and create reasons to support something you don't agree with, it's probably more fun for you than for your audience. Save the

A speechmaker's mission may be to inform or persuade, or both. Here Hillary Clinton speaks about health care reform to the United States Congress.

devil's advocate role for some other occasion and choose a topic you care about.

When you've got your subject, ask yourself what you would like to have your audience believe or do when the speech is finished—that is, what do you want to persuade them to do? By talking about subjects that touch the lives of your audience closely, by persuading them about situations in which they can have an impact, you create a better opportunity to give a gripping speech.

This doesn't mean you can't talk about big issues; you will just need to relate them to the lives of the people in your audience. If you are speaking about implementing a fair policy for organ transplants, for example, make sure your audience understands the importance to them of correcting the current situation. And be sure you tell them what they can do about it. You could, for example, propose that they look into the possibility of carrying a universal organ donor card in their own wallets, or suggest they write to their representatives in Congress, presenting their views.

You can argue that America should stop spending more than it has, or that the countries of the world should ban the bomb. Just make sure you let your audience know what part they can play, and what's in it for them. If you can't, consider tackling an issue closer to home: persuade your audience how important it is to develop a lifelong interest in sports, or to eat right, or to preserve First Amendment rights in the school newspaper.

Remember that in persuasive speeches, you can appeal to reason or to the emotions—or better yet, you can appeal to both. But first you need a topic both you and your audience can feel connected to and care about.

YOUR CHOICE

Having total freedom to choose a topic is either the best or worst situation to be in. It's clearly the best if you're very sure about what you want to say. It can be the worst if you feel you have so much to say, about so many things, that you can't quite bring the subject into focus. It can also be the worst if you feel you just have nothing to say.

As with narrowing down assigned topics, there are a few basic rules that might help:

- Choose a topic that interests you.
- Choose a topic you know something about.
- Choose a topic that you have strong feelings about.
- Choose a topic that suits your time limits.
- Decide whether your purpose is to persuade, to inform, or to entertain.
- Pick a topic you can research and write about in the time available to you.
- Develop an angle that you can speak from. Nurture a point of view.
- Pick a topic that will appeal to your audience.

STATING YOUR TOPIC

Once you've selected a topic, state it in a way that you can work with. It should no longer be "Baseball," though it might be "Why Women Should Play in the Major Leagues." It should not be "Graduation," though it might be "Education: A Life's Work." State your topic clearly, briefly, strongly, and in a way that expresses your feelings, thoughts, and opinions about the subject and at the same time appeals to your audience.

There are two ways to choose a title for your topic. Usually the nature of the topic itself suggests a title. Sometimes, however, coming up with a clever title helps the speechmaker to decide exactly what to talk about. For example, a fiction writer was asked to speak at a public library on the creative process. She knew the topic was too large, and puzzled about how to limit it to something that would interest both her and her audience. After a few days' thought, she came up with a title for her speech: "Using Other People's Lives." The title suggested the topic: the difference between writing fiction and writing a memoir, a narrative based on personal experience. Once she had the title, the speech seemed easy to research and write.

Once you've arrived at your topic, think seriously about your audience. Who they are, what they know and don't know about your subject, how they feel about it, and what brought them to your speech in the first place will all influence both the research you do, and the way your speech takes shape.

THREE

ASSESSING YOUR AUDIENCE

The best audience is one that is intelligent, well-educated—and a little drunk.

—Alben W. Barkley

Witticisms aside, the best audience is one you have taken the time to get to know. Who they are, what they know, how they feel about your subject, what they have been doing before and what they will be doing after your speech—all these factors will color the way you present your topic.

During the 1992 presidential race, for example, candidates Bill Clinton and then-president George Bush spoke to the American Legion Convention on the same day. The audience consisted for the most part of veterans of the Armed Forces. They were known to be extremely patriotic and overall to approve more of President Bush, who had served in combat in World War II, than of Bill Clinton, who was rumored to have avoided the draft during the Vietnam War.

President Bush spoke first. He wore his American Legion cap as he entered the auditorium, signifying that he was a member of this club. In his speech, Bush emphasized his war record: "I was scared, but I was willing. I was young, but I was ready. I had barely lived, when I began to watch men die."

Bush promised to clear up questions about prisoners of war and those missing in action in Vietnam. He was presented with the legion's Lifetime Achievement Award.

Clinton reasonably expected the audience to be less friendly toward him than they were toward President Bush. He knew he had to defend the fact that he did not fight in the war in Vietnam, and that he had never served in the Armed Forces. Clinton did not apologize; that might have made him appear weak. Instead, he explained the actions he had taken and the feelings he had had during the Vietnam War years. He also raised an issue he knew would be on the minds of the audience: whether a person who had never served in the military could be qualified to serve as commander in chief of the Armed Forces (one of the president's roles). Clinton cited several examples of presidents who had led the country in war but had never served in a war themselves: Abraham Lincoln, Woodrow Wilson, Franklin Roosevelt, and Ronald Reagan.

Both Bush and Clinton had done their homework. Even though they spoke to the same audience, it was a different audience for each of them. They tailored their speeches to fit. Both men received warm applause from the audience. And, in November 1992, Clinton won a larger share of the veterans' vote than Bush did.

How do you tailor your words to suit your listeners? It may help if you think of your speech as a product you are selling to your audience. Successful companies don't just dream up ideas, spend millions to produce them, and then introduce the results. First they do market research to ensure that what they make will meet buyers' needs.

Companies spend millions of dollars every year on surveys, and more millions on test marketing, to discover what people want, how much they want it, how much they are willing to pay for it, and how often they

*Assessing your audience: Jesse Jackson,
an effective speaker, tailors his choice
of subject, his language, and even his
posture to the audience—in this case,
a group of young students.*

would buy it. These facts are collected, analyzed, studied, reported on, and verified long before the first product makes it to the production line.

To prepare for "selling" your speech to your audience you will need to do some research before writing it. You can't sit down with your audience beforehand to ask what they think of your topic, but you can think about who these listeners will be, what mood they will be in, and the conditions under which they will be listening to you. You can follow up by talking in advance with a few audience members to focus your topic and presentation so that it has the best chance of being "bought," that is, avidly listened to.

When thinking about your audience, begin with the reporter's five questions: who? what? when? where? and why?

Who will be in the audience? Be specific. Adults, teenagers, or children, or a mixture of all three? You would use different language when addressing the third grade on voting than when addressing the League of Women Voters.

Will the audience be all male, all female, or a mixture? And, if a mixture, what proportion of each? Like most sensitive speakers, you will avoid making sexist remarks—comments that could insult men or women by their very nature—but you may want to vary the statistics, examples, or anecdotes you include in your speech based on the male/female ratio.

Is your expected audience a large or a small group? Small groups tend to be more intimate, to pay closer attention, and to share opinions. Large groups are more diverse, and you may need more compelling examples, language, imagery, and style to keep their attention. What do they already know and believe about your topic? Are you speaking about stamp collecting to your speech class, or to a group of philatelists? Do you need to establish that baseball is a sport, or can you get right to the fine points of pitching? Are they inclined to agree with you, or are they definitely on the other side of the fence? The amount of information they already have about your subject, as well as their assumptions and prejudices, will shape the structure of your speech and determine the level of detail you will need to include.

What issues or concerns will your audience have about your topic? How can you address these? What examples can you find that will calm their fears?

When will you be speaking? Are you first on the agenda, or last? Who else is speaking, and how will their topics relate to yours? Will you speak after dinner, when everyone is a little sleepy, or first thing in the morning, when most minds are at their most alert? After-dinner speeches need to be a little lighter, more entertaining, than early-morning presentations.

In fact, after-dinner speakers have almost a responsibility to be humorous. The morning audience is better equipped to absorb intricate and detailed information. After-lunch talks should mix solid information with some humor. Beware the mid- or late-afternoon audience: they may be far too tired to take in much of what you have to say.

Think, too, about the time of year. Your speech class will have a different atmosphere on the first day of school than it will an hour before spring break begins.

Where will you be speaking? Will you be in a classroom, onstage in an auditorium, in a television studio, in a restaurant, or outdoors at a graduation? Think about how your audience will feel. Will they be comfortable or ill at ease? Consider factors such as weather, restaurant noise, and other events that may be going on around you.

Why have they come: because they want to, or because they have to? Will they be eager to hear your speech, or are they captives who will need to be enter-

The Importance of Assessing Your Audience—An Example

Five high school seniors at a medium-size private school were asked to speak to a group of prospective students and their parents. One spoke only about his family; the audience yawned. The second spoke about the sports program, and a small part of the audience listened. The third talked about why she left the school in tenth grade and then returned to it; fidgeting was widespread. The fourth discussed her favorite teachers, and some people stood as if to leave.

But the fifth speaker caught the audience's attention. He spoke about how he felt at a meeting just like this one four years earlier. He talked about the questions he had then: Will I fit in? Will I get a good education? Will I have a good time, and still get into a good college? He told the audience the answers he had learned over the four years he'd been at the school. He told why he was glad he had chosen this school, especially now that he was about to leave for college. By giving his audience what they came for, he became the most successful speaker.

tained and enticed into listening? What does your audience hope to gain from your talk: information, an impassioned opinion, or half an hour's entertainment? While you don't want to pander to your audience, you will be a more effective speaker if you try to give them something of what they came for.

After the five W's, ask yourself one more reporter's question: how? How would you feel in their place?

Empathize with your audience. Write the speech that you would want to hear if you were sitting out there with them.

TALKING TO THE AUDIENCE

Go beyond imagining how your audience might feel: locate a few members of your audience, if possible, and ask them. You can ask members of your speech class to give you some advice on an upcoming speech, for example. Or discuss your valedictory address with a few of your classmates around the lunch table. If you don't know anyone who will be in your audience, ask the sponsor of the event to put you in touch with a few people who will be there. Three to five people will be more than enough.

Tell the audience members you locate that you want to know what topics they're interested in and what issues are on their minds. Mention your chosen topic, and determine if it's something they care about. If so, find out what angles they're interested in.

Ask open-ended questions. Don't ask if they'd be interested in hearing about baseball. Instead, ask what aspect of the recent player's strike interested them. Ask why they think women should or should not be allowed to play in the major leagues. Ask if there are any open issues that they'd like to hear more about. You'll be amazed at how glad people are to give their opinion.

Take notes. When you speak to the next person, see if he or she is interested in the same items as the previous person, or different ones.

If you can't find anyone who will be in your audience, or you're too shy to try it, how about talking with people you know who have things in common with your audience? For a speech to an audience of working women, for example, one female executive polled her friends on her topic: how women aged thirty and older felt about their jobs. Her friends, of course, were happy to talk to her.

The executive used the information she gathered to target her speech, and as research material. She reported in her speech, for instance, that more than half of the women she interviewed said they loved their jobs most of the time. And she told her audience that when women didn't like their jobs, there were three main reasons: too much responsibility without authority, too little pay, and not enough recognition. Because she had researched her audience thoroughly, the speech was easy to write.

WIIFM—OR "WHAT'S IN IT FOR ME?"

Before you begin to write your speech, ask yourself, If I were a member of my audience, what would be in it for me? What would I get out of this speech that would be valuable and useful to me?

Make sure you can answer this question. Whether it's information they can use, a joke they can repeat, a way to make a profit, or a new way to think about solving old problems, make sure that your audience gets to take away something they want.

WHAT DO YOU WANT TO ACCOMPLISH?

Now that you've considered your audience, and what they want, consider what effect you want to have on them. Do you want to meet their expectations, or surprise them? Satisfy their curiosity, or generate more questions? Motivate them to take action, or talk them out of doing something they seem hell-bent on anyway?

Knowing both what you want to accomplish and what your audience wants and needs to hear will give you considerable guidance in the next step: doing your research.

36

FOUR

RESEARCHING YOUR TOPIC

*Knowledge is of two kinds: we know a subject
ourselves, or we know where we can find
information upon it.*

—Samuel Johnson

GETTING STARTED

If you've chosen or narrowed your topic wisely, you already know something about it. Begin by making a written inventory of the facts, opinions, and feelings you have on hand, that is, everything you know or think you know about your subject. Taking stock this way will give you a good idea of what you still need to know and how to find it.

Putting your ideas on paper will also help you get a clear picture of what they are. Sometimes you won't know what you're thinking until you start to put it into words. Other times, what seemed like a good idea in your head turns out to be fuzzy and unclear when it appears on paper.

Writing your ideas also helps you see how your thoughts relate to one another, what points you can already support with facts, and where you need additional information.

You might find it useful to write your ideas on note cards. Choose a size that is small enough to carry around but big enough to really write on. For most

37

people 4- by 6-inch cards work well, though you may prefer larger cards, such as 5 by 8.

Write notes only on one side of the card. When you are hunting for a fact you remember copying but can't find, you will at least know that it is not on the back of any of your cards.

Use one card for each idea. Try to state each thought you have about your subject as fully as possible. Add supporting evidence, however sketchy, under the idea, like this:

When young people drink alcohol, the consequences can be serious.

Many teenagers I know drink heavily.

People who drink too much lose control of themselves.

Underage drinking is illegal, but it seems that few people are ever punished for it. Why isn't the law enforced?

You don't need facts to support these thoughts, observations, and assumptions—not yet, anyway. Consider them as clues to the facts you will need to find.

If an idea expands to take up more than a single card, be sure to number the cards for that idea as you fill them. That way, it will be easier to deal with the facts you have gathered later on.

When you have written out everything you already think, know, and feel about your topic, take some time to read over your ideas. Sort through them slowly, making additional notes as they come to mind. Underline the ideas which seem strongest, clearest, most useful: the words that have some power for you. These are the seeds from which your speech will grow. Copy them onto fresh cards, writing strong simple sentences and stating your ideas as clearly as possible:

Teenage drinking is a major problem in our community.

Teen drinking is illegal.

Some parents let their kids have parties where beer and wine are served.

Heavy drinking can lead to automobile accidents and death.

If some of your key ideas contradict each other, don't worry. In fact, it is a good sign—it means your ideas are lively and in motion, that you are thinking creatively and from several angles about your topic. You can sort out the contradictions later, after you've done your research. For now, simply formulate assertions:

Students' First Amendment rights are threatened by the school board's censorship of the high school paper.

Perennials are the backbone of the English floral border.

Robots improve both our technological processes and the products they manufacture.

Write down opposing opinions as they come to mind, too. Answering objections is important in certain types of speeches, and you can't answer them if you don't know what they are:

Student publications aren't covered by the First Amendment of the U.S. Constitution.

Although colorful, perennials bloom only for a short time.

Robots are taking jobs away from human workers.

By now, you should have some idea of the kinds of information you need. Use your index cards to make a list of the information you're after. Is it a book about robots, or statistics on unemployment and its causes? Are you trying to find an article on baseball players you saw a few weeks ago in either *Time* or *Sports Illustrated*? Do you think you'd like a quote from some famous English gardener to support some of your own observations? Maybe you'd like statistics on teenage drinking and its consequences to help make your points.

Make a list of what you'd like or need to know. Be as specific as you can. Don't worry if your list isn't complete or entirely clear; part of the fun of research is stumbling across unexpected, interesting, useful information while you're hot on the trail of something else entirely.

Before you head to the library, take a look around your room and your home. If you've chosen a topic that interests you, you probably have some basic material at hand: a favorite gardening book, say, or copies of *Sports Illustrated* that contain articles related to your topic. Begin to gather your materials in a single place, a folder, a drawer, a corner of your desk or floor.

Whether you need quotes from major-league players, union leaders' pronouncements on the use of robots in Detroit, the text of the First Amendment, a list of perennial plants, or data on teenage drinking and driving, your next stop should be the library.

USING THE LIBRARY AND OTHER RESOURCES

The best source of information in most libraries is not a book, a magazine, an index, an abstract, or a piece of microfilm. It is a human being, the librarian. Try talking to your librarian before you dive into the card catalog or *The Readers' Guide to Periodical Literature*. Chances

The librarian, an invaluable guide to the resources of the library

are, the librarian will be pleased to help and will speed your search for information.

Begin by introducing yourself. "Hi, I'm _____, I'm a student at _____, and I have to make a speech on _____. I need to find _____." Show the librarian your list, and you will soon find yourself delving into some of the following sources of information. If your librarian can't help you, search out these sources for yourself.

Encyclopedias

Encyclopedias provide the big picture on a variety of topics, and can help you get a quick overview of the subject you have chosen. General encyclopedias include the *Americana,* the *Britannica,* and *Collier's.* These are written for the general reader, so they are easy to understand and may contain facts you can use easily.

More specialized encyclopedias, such as *The Encyclopedia of Textiles, The Encyclopedic Dictionary of Physics,* or *The Encyclopedia of Pop Music,* are better bets for specialized information. In some cases the material may be more difficult for the general reader to understand, but it will be complete, detailed, and specific. Encyclopedias exist on almost every topic you can imagine. They are useful places to begin research.

Yearbooks

In addition to their standard A-to-Z volumes, many encyclopedias issue annual yearbooks, which supplement and update the basic volumes. These are especially helpful if you are concerned with recent developments in a particular field.

The *Statistical Abstract of the United States* is another useful yearbook. Published by the U.S. Bureau of the Census, it contains a wealth of facts, tables, graphs, and statistics on subjects including population, education, science, energy, and many, many more. A similar book, published by the United Nations and called *The Statistical Yearbook*, offers similar information on more than 150 countries around the world.

The *Facts On File Yearbook* is also handy. You can check news summaries of the great events of a given year, or read week-by-week detailed accounts of major news items. If you're following the events of the Korean War, for example, or Harry Truman's presidency, *Facts On File* can very helpful.

Almanacs

Almanacs contain lists, charts, and other types of factual information, usually from a variety of fields. The best known is *The World Almanac and Book of Facts*. It is beautifully indexed and contains an incredible assortment of information. Check it out.

Indexes

Indexes are your door into the vast array of periodical literature, that is, the magazines and newspapers that day after day, month after month, and year after year supply the general reader with current information on a broad range of topics.

The Readers' Guide to Periodical Literature lists information on articles in more than 100 American commercial periodicals that address a general audience. Articles are indexed by both subject and author (not by title). Entries will tell you all you need to find the article you're looking for: title of the article, the author's name, the magazine the article appeared in, and the date, volume number, and page number of the magazine.

The New York Times Index will help you find information that has been published in *The New York Times* during the last 100-plus years. Major news stories are summarized in the *Index,* so even if your library can't put a set of *New York Times* microfilms at your disposal, the *Index* itself can be very useful.

Microfilms and Microfiche

Some documents, such as collections of newspapers, would be difficult for a library to store. They are bulky, and the paper on which they are printed disintegrates quickly.

That's why many libraries store copies of newspapers and other documents on microfilm or microfiche. Documents on microfilm or microfiche are greatly reduced in size, making it easy to keep large quantities of information in a small space. And the film on which they are printed, if properly stored, lasts far longer than paper.

Microfilm readers are available in libraries that store documents on film or fiche. These readers enlarge the text and photographs and project them onto a screen that is fairly easy to read. If you are looking for contemporary newspaper stories about women's suffrage, the sinking of the *Titanic*, or other historical events, ask your librarian if microfilm of *The New York Times* or other newspapers of the day is available.

On-line Information

These days, computers can help you find the information you are looking for. In many libraries, a computerized service lets you locate books by subject, title, or author, and will even tell you where the book you want is located.

In addition, there are several on-line search services that will allow you to find data right from your terminal at home. LEXIS, for legal information, and NEXIS, for news, are perhaps the best-known computerized services. If you are connected to an electronic information service such as Prodigy or CompuServe, you may have access to research materials over the wires.

Sources for Quotations

Every good library will carry several source books of quotations. The most widely available and perhaps most widely quoted source is *Bartlett's Familiar Quotations*. Check both older editions and the latest version, the sixteenth edition, published in 1992. While older editions tend to contain quotations that are overused, overly literary, or overly long for inclusion in speeches, the sixteenth edition offers pithy quotes from Bud Abbott to Émile Zola, on just about any topic you can name.

Several more contemporary collections of quotations might prove even more useful. These are usually available at bookstores in inexpensive paperback editions, so if your local or school library does not have the one you are looking for, you may want to buy it. These books include:

- *Peter's Quotations: Ideas for Our Time,* edited by Dr. Laurence J. Peter. This is full of varied and witty sayings. You can find quotes from Woody Allen ("I'm not afraid to die; I just don't want to be there when it happens"), Joe Namath, and Albert Einstein on topics ranging from ability to zoos.
- The *Barnes & Noble Book of Quotations,* edited by Robert I. Fitzhenry. In this useful source you'll find Gilda Radner quoted on the same page with Voltaire, and the subjects run from ability and achievement to youth. This collection includes many national proverbs—such as the Irish saying "Better quarreling than lonesome," or the Dutch "A handful of patience is worth more than a bushel of brains"—that can be fun to use.
- *The Great Thoughts,* compiled by George Seldes. Unfortunately, this book is arranged by author, not by subject, so, while you might want to browse in it, finding something that relates to your topic can be a matter of luck.
- *The Beacon Book of Quotations by Women,* compiled by Rosalie Maggio. Here you'll find quotes from more than 1,300 women on more than 800 subjects, including Erica Jong on talent ("Everyone has talent. What is rare is the courage to follow the talent to the dark place

where it leads"), Mary Mapes Dodge on Holland ("The entire country is a kind of saturated sponge"), and Dorothy Parker on dogma ("You can't teach an old dogma new tricks").

Anecdotes

In speeches, anecdotes are useful to illustrate a point, but a good anecdote is hard to find. Keep your eyes and ears open, though, as you read, watch television, or listen to the radio, and you'll begin to see that good anecdotes are everywhere. It's finding the one you need when you need it that's difficult.

Try a collection of anecdotes, such as *The Little, Brown Book of Anecdotes,* edited by Clifton Fadiman. The stories are arranged according to their subject, and if you are looking for anecdotes about Abraham Lincoln, for example, or Albert Einstein, or Yogi Berra, you might find just what you need.

Humor

Jokes, like anecdotes, are rarely around when you need them. But there are some good sources for humorous ideas you can modify and put to use, including:

- *The Big Book of American Humor,* edited by William Novak and Moshe Waldoks. This includes compilations of lawyer jokes, elephant jokes, and lightbulb jokes, as well as humor by Russell Baker, Lily Tomlin, Garrison Keillor, and others. While you won't find a joke for every occasion, you will find lots of useful ideas.
- *The Penguin Dictionary of Modern Humorous Quotations,* compiled by Fred Metcalf. Like many books of quotations, this is arranged by topic. However, here all the quotations are humorous, such as W. C. Fields's famous line, "A woman drove me to drink and I never even had the courtesy to thank her."

- Humor magazines. One called *Funny Times,* published monthly, is a good source for political humor.

Additional Sources

If you're giving a speech in a particular spot and need to know more about it, you can obtain information from the local chamber of commerce, or consult a travel guide to learn more about the place.

Consider wandering through the reference section of your library and taking a good look at what's on the shelves. You may come across just what you're looking for: *A Dictionary of Greek and Roman Biography and Mythology, Contemporary Poets, American Women Poets,* or *The Motion Picture Guide.*

Books

For current topics, such as drug testing, rock music, or the growth of the computer chip industry, books might be less useful than periodicals. It just takes longer to get a good book into print than it does to publish a magazine article, and much of the information you find in books on really hot topics may be less than fresh.

In addition, as with most speeches, you are probably writing yours against a deadline, so you may not have time to read an entire book or two before you make your speech.

But if you're looking for the historical background on a current social, political, or economic problem, or even on such subjects as gardening, computers, robots, or space exploration, you may wish to read a book or two to give yourself a sense of the context in which current events are taking place.

Use the card catalog to find books on the subject you're interested in. Some libraries still have cards in drawers, and some publish card catalogs as a series of paperback books, but the most up-to-date libraries make their card catalogs available through computer

With access to an on-line catalog, library researchers can locate exactly the material they need to construct a convincing speech.

terminals, on-line. In all cases, books are listed by subject, by the author's last name, and by title. All the lists are in alphabetic order. If you need help learning to navigate through your library's catalog, ask your librarian.

Video- and Audiotapes

Many libraries now stock video- and audiocassette tapes, and if your topic is business-related or deals with the entertainment industry, if the visual aspect is important—as in sculpture or painting—videotapes and audiotapes may be the sources you need. Many topics have been covered in how-to tapes—everything from how to dress for success to cooking a soufflé to closing a sale. If your topic is covered by a tape, find the time to look at one.

AFTER YOU'VE FOUND YOUR SOURCES

Now that you've located the books, magazines, or videotapes you need, read through or view your material and make notes on the facts that will help you write a convincing speech.

Use your index cards, one for each source. At the top of the card, list the name of the book or magazine, the date of issue, the page number(s) you're working from, and any other reference material you would need (such as library call numbers) to locate that piece of information again. Write all this down before you make a single note.

You may be tempted to skip this step; don't. It is amazing how many times you'll need to go back and check your sources, and if you are not rigorous about noting bibliographical information, tracking down a once-found fact a second time may prove difficult.

Once you've identified your source on the card, jot down the facts, quotes, anecdotes, or examples you find useful. You may wish to write the facts in your own words, or you may want to copy the language exactly as it's written so that you can quote it word for word. If you copy exactly, make sure you put quotation marks around your notes, so you won't forget that you've quoted.

RESTATING YOUR TOPIC

When you've completed your research, you may discover that your topic, or the angle you've chosen, looks different to you. You may have uncovered information which changes your outlook. Or you may have discovered that no information is available on exactly the angle you want to speak about, but that a slightly different topic has been suggested by the material you did find.

Now is the time to restate your topic, to put it into its final form based on what you've learned from your research. Try not to go after a new topic entirely, but alter your statement of theme as much as necessary. "Why Women Should Be Playing Major-League Ball," may turn into "Why Women Have Been Shut Out of Major-League Baseball." "Why Drug Testing Should Be Mandatory in Our School District" might become, as a result of your research, "Drug Testing for Teenagers: Pro and Con." "Why Teenagers Shouldn't Drink" might become "How Advertising Encourages Teen Drinking."

Make whatever changes you need in your topic statement so that you can write a speech you believe in and one that your audience can believe, one based on research and evidence. Recast your title, if you need to, so that it reflects your new slant.

50

FIVE

OUTLINES AND DRAFTS

*Writing is the hardest way of earning a living, with
the possible exception of wrestling alligators.*

—Olin Miller

Most people who take long car trips consult a map
before they set out. They consider, at least vaguely, the
route they will take. Others, of course, map out their
journey in detail. Still others just take to the road, head-
ing in the general direction of their destination and
putting their faith in the signs they expect to find along
the way.

Outlines are not speeches, and writing an outline
may not help you to write a speech. But sometimes
teachers require outlines of what you plan to say. Other
times, you may want to create an outline to serve as a
kind of road map, a plan that tells you where you want
to go and how, approximately, you'll get there. Other
times, you may want to plunge right into the writing and
set your thoughts in order as you go, or after you've
written it all out.

If you need or want to create an outline for your
speech, write your topic statement at the top of a clean
sheet of paper. Then look through your idea and note
cards and group your supporting ideas together. Begin
to build an outline by writing down the major points that

support your topic statement. Leave room to fill in details—examples, facts, quotes—that bolster each of your stated opinions. And don't forget to state objections and answer them.

Once you have a basic framework in place, you can fill in more details to create an outstanding outline. Or you can use your framework as the basis for a first draft.

Whether you plan to read your speech, speak from note cards, or deliver your thoughts from memory, it's a good idea to write down your speech. Many ideas will not crystallize unless they are forced onto paper, into words. Once your ideas are on the page, you can and will be able to take a good, hard look at them, study them, push them around until they say exactly what you mean.

And it is always easier to speak, even if you work from notes or from memory, if you have already prepared a text of your speech. You will remember connections better. Working your ideas through on paper will give you a sense of how your argument builds.

But what if, like many writers, often even experienced professionals, you have trouble getting started?

ELIMINATING WRITER'S BLOCK

You say the sight of a blank sheet of paper scares you? You're blocked, you're blank, you can't think of how to begin or, once you begin, can't think of what to say next? Welcome to the writer's world.

Even experienced writers can suffer something like terror when faced with a blank page. It is scary to write. Part of the fear comes from facing the unknown: you really don't know what you are going to say until you say it. Another part of the anxiety might come from the feeling that whatever you put down won't be good enough—and not necessarily for other people, but not good enough for the critical side of you.

52

Many writers talk about the writing process as if they were in fact two people: a writer and an editor. Whatever words the writer puts on the page, the editor always manages to find fault with them. "That's silly!" the editor says. "You can't start with *I*! You don't know what you're doing. What makes you think you can write a good speech?"

If these sound like voices you've heard in your head when you sit down to write, take heart. Your editor, the critical part of you that keeps you from writing, is a handy sort to have around—once the actual writing is done and the revising and editing have started. You will need that critical awareness to find and remove excess language, insert commas, and generally determine whether you are communicating effectively through the words you've chosen.

But during the process of setting words down on paper the editor is no help. So tell that critical part of you to take a hike, take a nap, or take a vacation until after you've written your first draft. Until that draft exists completely, you are only a writer, involved in putting your ideas into words and setting those words on a page.

If your editor is persistent and nagging, as many are, you may have to resort to some time-honored tricks to shake off this critic long enough to write. Here are two that have worked for professional writers and may work for you.

Writing Before the Critic Is Awake

Get up in the morning an hour earlier than usual and go directly to your desk or other work area. Write everything you know about your speech without stopping. Get out as much as you can. If this works but you don't get it all down in one day, try it again on successive mornings.

Be careful not to read or listen to the radio or watch television before you begin. You don't want the critic to wake up before you get as many words on the page as possible. Don't worry about whether the words are the perfect ones or if you're writing everything in exactly the order you should. If you have an outline, follow it loosely, letting yourself stray as much as you want to, pulling yourself gently back to the subject at hand if you think you have wandered too far afield.

Tiring Out the Critic

If you can't get up before your critic is awake, try tiring out your critic. First make sure your work area is ready for you. Set out paper and pens or pencil, get your typewriter ready or your computer in order—whatever tools you need to write. If you're using an outline, look it, over reading it to yourself several times. Then set it down, and leave the house.

Indulge in some solitary sport for at least an hour. Take a long walk, or jog, or swim, or roller-skate— whatever appeals to you. Keep your topic gently in mind as you exercise, but don't force yourself to think of it. During the last part of the hour and as you head back to your desk or other workplace, picture yourself sitting down and effortlessly writing everything you know about your topic.

When you reach your prepared workplace, sit down and begin to write immediately. Put everything you know about your speech down on paper. Again, don't worry if what you write sounds silly or confused. You'll straighten it out during the revision process. Drafts can always be improved, as long as they exist. Getting something down, no matter how small a corner of your ideas, gives you a way into the rest of them. Just write.

If you have no quiet place to work at home, plan to end up at a library. Carry your notebook or pad and pens and pencils with you. When you arrive, find a spot quickly, sit down, and begin to write immediately.

ELIMINATING PROCRASTINATION

Suppose you don't have a problem writing once you get started, but starting—well, you never seem to get around to it. Maybe you put off writing until the last minute, telling yourself you work better under pressure and leaving barely enough time to write a first draft, let alone revise and polish it.

If that pattern sounds familiar, you suffer from procrastination. It can be cured. The simplest way is just to constantly say to yourself, "Do it now!" Whatever "it" is—walking the dog, reading a book, taking out the recyclables—just do it. When it's time to write, *do it now!*

Another way to break through stalling involves working with a kitchen timer. Pick a small amount of time, ten to twenty minutes. Set the timer and promise yourself you will write without stopping until the bell rings.

If doesn't matter if you spend the first few minutes writing nonsense; that often happens. If you keep putting one word after another on the paper, writing without a pause, you will eventually come around to your subject. And once you've begun, it will be easier to go on. Remember, don't stop until the bell rings.

When your time is up, stop writing and reward yourself. Take a walk, have a snack, watch part of a favorite TV show, or listen to some music—whatever gives you pleasure. Then set the timer again for another session and write. Do as many short sessions as it takes you to get a complete first draft on the page. After the first few sessions, you may find yourself so engaged with your topic that you will work on past the timer.

Sometimes people procrastinate because the job at hand seems overwhelming. If that's the problem, break the task down into smaller segments. Write the opening in one session, write the close another time,

*An eloquent and powerful speaker,
Dr. Martin Luther King, Jr., captured
the full attention of a vast assembly
at the 1963 March on Washington
civil rights demonstration.*

and fill in the middle in a third session. Or try writing all the transitions, the sentences that take you from one topic to another. Later you can fill in the details.

Another way to work is to type up your speech outline, leaving lots of white space. Then tell yourself you are going to make notes only on the outline. As you go through the outline, jot down the relevant ideas and facts that occur to you. You don't have to be precise; just give yourself enough information so you'll know what you mean when you look at it later. Then retype the outline, adding all your handwritten notes, and begin the process again. By adding more detail each time you go through your outline, you will soon build up the body of your speech.

Whatever method you choose to get your first draft down on paper, work regularly; then reward yourself for your accomplishment.

BUILDING SELF-CONFIDENCE

If lack of self-confidence keeps you from writing, give yourself positive messages instead of the negative ones you're probably working from now. Tell yourself you can do it. Repeat to yourself, as often as possible, encouraging words such as "I can write this speech. I know a lot about my subject."

You don't have to believe the positive messages you send yourself. They'll work if you keep repeating them, whether you believe them or not.

NOW THAT YOU'RE READY TO WRITE

You have your outline prepared. You know your main ideas, and the order in which they should appear. You've planned, if necessary, to outsmart your critic, work through your procrastination, and build your confidence. But how do you actually put your ideas into words?

There is a simple time-tested formula for giving a speech, and here it is. It may sound boring, it may sound old-fashioned, but it never fails. Every speech has three parts:

1. A beginning
2. A middle, or body
3. An end, or close

Each part of the speech serves a clear and necessary function:

1. The beginning: tell them what you are going to tell them
2. The middle: tell them
3. The end: tell them what you've told them

That's it. If it sounds easy, it is. Here's how it works in more detail.

TELL THEM WHAT YOU ARE GOING TO TELL THEM: THE BEGINNING

What does it mean to tell your audience what you're going to tell them?

You could say, "Today I'm going to talk about teenage drinking and how advertising encourages it." And if you did, it would be a clear, simple, and direct beginning.

But would it get your audience's attention? Would it arouse their interest, perk up their ears, and make them want to hear more? Probably not. And arousing your audience's interest is exactly what the opening of your speech should do: while it states your topic, it should also create an appetite in your listeners for the rest of the speech.

Because your first sentences will prepare the audience for what is to follow, much as an appetizer prepares you for the dinner that is to come, it pays to give your opening a great deal of thought. Usually, you won't be able to write a strong opening until after you have completed a first draft. Or as one student put it, "How can I know how to prepare the audience for what's to come when I don't even know what's coming yet?"

That being the case, you may want to begin your first draft with that uninspiring opening, "Today I am going to talk about . . . " and go back and rewrite the opening later. Or you may want to begin by considering one of these tried-and-true ways of opening a speech.

Use a Quote

Sometimes the best words to begin with belong to someone else. Quotes can be gripping, amusing, naughty, or shocking. You can quote from one of your sources, from an expert in your field, or from a famous wit—Will Rogers, Oscar Wilde, or Gilda Radner. If you do quote from a public figure famous for using language well, but not necessarily well versed in your topic, be sure to connect the saying back to your subject and your point of view.

You can quote someone you agree with or someone you think is all wrong. But whomever you quote, choose carefully, always keeping in mind your audience and the effect you wish to have on them.

Sometimes the most unlikely sources of sayings can be used to make a point. One successful writer began a speech on international marketing by quoting a person he identified as "a very successful market analyst." "I don't even know what street Canada is on," this famous marketeer was quoted as saying. What gave the opening its punch? The revelation that the words belonged to Al Capone.

You don't have to use a quote that deals directly

with your subject. Just make sure the quote can be tied to your subject—and make sure you provide the link.

Think, too, about the kind of people you want to quote. A speechwriter trying to explain why a product that had been announced years before was just coming to market used a quote, "Anything worth doing is worth doing slowly." It was cut from the speech because the source turned out to be the famous stripteaser Gypsy Rose Lee.

In his speech to the 1992 Republican National Convention, President George Bush quoted Harry Truman. Harry Truman was a Democrat; and when Truman ran for the presidency in 1948, George Bush, a Republican, probably voted for his opponent, Thomas Dewey. The choice of the source seemed peculiar, and weakened the president's speech.

If you expect your audience might be a little groggy after lunch, you could use a quote that will shock—and then disagree with it. For instance, you might begin a speech supporting the idea of a military draft by quoting Emma Goldman, an anarchist and antimilitary service agitator, who said, "All wars are wars among thieves who are too cowardly to fight and who therefore induce the young manhood of the whole world to do the fighting for them." You could then go on to differ with Goldman and present your ideas of why it is important to keep a standing army and why a draft is the best way to do it.

Books of quotations aren't the only sources of quotable material. Listen to political speeches, read current magazines and cartoons, and listen to comedians. Proverbs also make good quotes to open speeches, as do tag lines from current or well-known television commercials.

Ronald Reagan was a master of quotation. In 1988, debating presidential candidate Walter Mondale, Reagan quoted a famous hamburger chain's commercial,

*Eleanor Roosevelt held her audience
with a straightforward delivery of
great warmth and sincerity.*

"Where's the beef?" And in his speech before the 1992 Republican convention, Reagan got laughs by updating a quote from a 1988 vice presidential debate. In 1988, Democratic vice presidential candidate Lloyd Bentsen had told his Republican opponent, Dan Quayle, "I knew John Kennedy. John Kennedy was a friend of mine. And believe me, you're no John Kennedy." In 1992, Reagan said, "I knew Thomas Jefferson. Thomas Jefferson was a friend of mine. And believe me, you're no Thomas Jefferson," and got a big laugh, because he was making fun of his own age.

Begin with Humor

Reagan's quote worked in part because he poked fun gently at himself. Ross Perot scored well in the 1992 presidential debates for the same reason: at one point, the billionaire told the audience he was "all ears." While he meant he was really listening, he was also mildly poking fun at his own appearance.

Audiences always appreciate and listen to humor. In fact, many people feel the only way to begin a speech is with a joke. Whether you open with humor is up to you. But if you do, make sure that your humor is closely tied to your subject, that it's really funny, and that you can deliver it well. Also, be careful to avoid jokes that are racist, sexist, ethnic, dirty, or ageist, that is, any joke that might offend all or part of your audience.

If you start with a joke, remember that its purpose is not to loosen up the audience or to prove that you are a likable person. Its function is to get your audience ready to hear the rest of what you have to say.

Gentle humor can work as well, if not better, than a joke with a punch line. For instance, one speaker began by telling the audience about some translation signs seen in foreign hotel lobbies. "Please enter the lift backwards, and only when lit up," one said. Another

Humor Without Hurt

How can you be sure the humor you use won't hurt anybody? Well, you can't be totally sure, but here are some guidelines for using humor without causing hurt.

1. *Kid people about what they kid themselves about.* Ronald Reagan makes jokes about his age. So does everyone else.
2. *Kid about things that don't matter.* Jay Leno makes jokes about Bill Clinton's love of Big Macs. Everyone made fun of Gerry Ford's golf game.
3. *Kid yourself.* One short man introduced himself to an audience as "vertically challenged." Another short man who holds a prominent government position often begins his speeches by saying, "And you thought I represented big government!"

said, "Please leave your values at the desk." The audience laughed, and nodded when the speaker went on to talk about preserving important company values, even in tough economic times.

Ask a Question

If your speech sets out to answer a specific question or set of questions, you can begin by asking them. "What drove America into World War II?" "Does a good president have to have military experience?" "Why are health care costs rising so quickly, and what can we do about them?" These are called rhetorical questions—questions to which no answer is expected, or to which only a single answer can be made.

Make sure your question is to the point, however, or you run the risk of being dismissed by the audience, as was Vice Admiral Stockdale, Ross Perot's running mate, who opened his 1992 vice presidential debate appearance with two questions he should not have had to ask: "Who am I? Why am I here?"

Tell an Anecdote

Anecdotes, short accounts of interesting or humorous incidents, can be effective openings. Where do you find good anecdotes? From your own experience, sometimes, or you can consult collections, although you may have to tailor what you find to fit your subject and your style. You can adopt a friend's story or one that happened to someone else, or one you read in a newspaper.

You can also create fictional anecdotes to make the points you need. Suppose you want to begin a speech against drug testing with an anecdote. You wish to illustrate the fact that drug tests are far from foolproof, that in fact they can give false results more often than people realize.

So you present an invented character: Melissa Jones, an honor student, editor of her school yearbook, head cheerleader. Well liked, smart, a good kid. Along with everyone else in her mythical high school, she is tested for drug use and the test shows cocaine in her system.

Her parents are stunned and distraught. She is thrown off the cheerleading squad, asked to resign from the yearbook. Her boyfriend drops her. Her friends' parents say she can't see them anymore. Doesn't the test prove she's on drugs?

Well, no. Eventually, the test is shown to have given a false positive. Melissa is cleared of the suspicion of using drugs, but meanwhile her life has been changed forever.

Having created an anecdote that engages your audience, you can then tell in less emotional terms why drug testing in your school is a bad idea.

Begin with Facts

A single surprising fact or a number of startling statistics that build to a climax can make your audience hungry to hear more. For a speech on the problem of teen drinking, for example, you might begin with any or all of the following facts:

> *According to government statistics, at least eight million American teenagers use alcohol every week, and almost half a million go on a weekly binge (or five drinks in a row).*

> *Junior and senior high school students drink 35 percent of all wine coolers sold in the United States—31 million gallons—and 1.1 billion cans of beer each year.*

> *The U.S. Department of Justice reports that almost one third of young people who commit serious crimes have consumed alcohol just before doing so.*

Where do you find interesting statistics? They are everywhere. But some of the funniest are reported each month in Harper's Index, published in *Harper's* magazine. For instance, did you know that there are 15,000 Avon ladies in China? Or that the amount spent on candy last Mother's Day, for each American mother, was nearly $5.00? It's the kind of information that can help you enter a speech with grace and humor.

Whatever statistics you choose, make sure they are compelling. Be certain they are accurate. And present facts in a way that makes them easy for readers to understand and to remember.

Round off numbers. For example, the exact amount spent on Mother's Day candy per mother was $4.70. "Nearly $5.00" is easier for an audience to hear.

Make numbers easy to see. If you're explaining how large scientists believe a dinosaur was, compare it to something else large—a two-story building or St. Patrick's Cathedral—that your audience can quickly picture.

Challenge an Assumption or Two

Because you've thought about your audience, you have some sense of what they assume. So you might begin your speech by challenging and overturning those assumptions.

For example, in a speech on how to improve American schools, you might open by challenging the commonly held belief that public schools are worse than they were fifty years ago. You could point out that fifty years ago fewer people finished high school; that scientific knowledge was less advanced, and hence less difficult to teach and to learn; that schools fifty years ago produced unskilled laborers and were pretty good at that. You could then demonstrate that what we need today, on the other hand, are skilled workers—and that's where the problem lies.

Instead of blaming schools, you could talk about how the role schools play in our society has changed. And then you could talk about the ways schools could be altered to make them better able to meet the needs of today's students, and today's jobs.

Once the audience has had its assumptions challenged, they are more likely to listen.

TELL THEM: THE BODY OF THE SPEECH

Now that your audience knows what you're talking about and is ready to hear more, it's time to present your main points, to make assertions backed by evidence.

There are as many ways to organize the body of a speech as there are topics. The one you select will depend both on your audience and your material. Consider a few of the possibilities.

Deductive and Inductive Approaches

Deduction and induction are two ways of presenting evidence and arriving at conclusions. You use the deductive method when you present your main idea up front and then provide the details. In inductive reasoning, you build your case by providing the details first, arriving at your main idea later. Inductive and deductive formats are often used in speeches that attempt to persuade.

The format you choose depends to a large extent on how you expect your audience to respond to your ideas. For example, let's suppose you are giving a speech against alcohol-industry advertising aimed at teenagers, and the members of your class are your audience. You suspect that many of your classmates enjoy drinking and won't like the message you've prepared. In that case, you would not begin by stating your opinion. To do so might alienate your audience; they might stop listening before you could state the reasons behind your stance.

Instead, you might decide to give your reasons, one by one, and build to your conclusion: that for reason A, reason B, and reason C, alcohol advertising aimed at teenagers is not a good idea and should not be allowed. By using the inductive format, you give yourself time to win your audience over a little, before you present an opinion that is different from their own.

But suppose you are instead speaking on the same topic to the school board, which is composed largely of adults who oppose teenage drinking. Using a deductive format, you let your audience know up front that you agree with them, then provide the reasons why.

Chronology

Some speeches, of course, are not persuasive. Instead they inform an audience about a set of facts. Or, within a persuasive speech, you may wish to trace the history or development of an attitude, an idea, or a situation.

In these cases, consider organizing the body of your speech chronologically, that is, in order of the time at which each event happened. Talks about the history of the designated hitter, the development of robotics, or the growth cycle of the redwood tree would all benefit from the use of chronological order.

While it's usually easy to organize information chronologically (this happened, then this, then that . . .), be aware that there are pitfalls. The biggest potential problem is dullness and predictability. Most people know that trees start from seeds, become seedlings, and grow bigger, or that the Great Depression came before World War II, which preceded the Baby Boom. To counteract the tendency toward predictability, use lively language and fresh examples.

You might also begin, as the epic poets did, at the climax of your story, in the middle of things. Then you can go back to the beginning and show the path of events and circumstances that led to that climax. For example, you might begin a speech on the causes of World War II with the bombing of Pearl Harbor, then backtrack to the end of World War I and the Treaty of Versailles, to show how that treaty engendered the next world war.

Cause and Effect

Another way to arrange the body of your speech is in terms of cause and effect. Tell your audience what events led to the current situation. For instance, if you are discussing events that led to the development of

*New York governor Mario Cuomo, a celebrated
public speaker, uses podium appearances to
present his positions and gain public
support for them.*

alternative energy sources, you might wish to mention
the Arab oil embargo of the early 1970s, which created
a shortage of oil products and higher prices. These
higher prices in turn affected the U.S. balance of pay-

ments and the growth of the U.S. economy and led to government tax incentives and credits for the development of solar, wind, and other energy sources.

Geographic Order

If your subject is the breakup of the Soviet Union, the location of factories or air bases, the movement of Haitian refugees toward the United States mainland, or any other topic grounded in geography, organize your material geographically.

Begin in the north and work south, or start in the east and work west, or, of course, vice versa. You can even begin in the center and work out, as long as you choose a starting point and announce your direction early in the speech. "I'll begin with the northern region, and work toward the south." This makes it easier for your audience to follow your words.

Quantitative Order

If you are discussing the ten biggest diamond deposits on Earth, you can begin with the largest and work toward the smallest, or vice versa. In general it's best to work from smallest to largest, from the least to most impressive. Think of it this way: if you start with the biggest, you can lose your audience's attention as you move down the line. If you start small and build, audience interest usually builds with you.

Vary the amount of time you spend on each element. And don't give exactly the same information about each point or you will surely bore your audience.

Transitions

No matter which way you choose to organize your material, you will need to move smoothly and strongly from one point to the next. Think of transitions as both signposts and bridges. Transitions tell your audience where you are in your speech, and lead them forward from one idea to the next. Consider some of the following:

Let's begin on the east coast. . . .
Moving now to the heartland . . .
Finally, in the far west . . .

First, think about the color of your garden. . . .
Second, give some thought to the height of the plants. . . .
Next, take season of bloom into account. . . .
Finally, map your garden on graph paper. . . .

The smallest of three major oil deposits is located . . .
The next largest deposit is . . .
But the most impressive reservoir can be found . . .

If you find yourself writing, or saying, things such as "I'd like to talk about the second largest diamond in the world, but before I do, let me digress . . ." go back and rethink the order of your speech. Weak, wordy transitions appear when something is in the wrong place. When ideas flow logically, you won't need a lot of words to get from one point to the next.

In addition to using obvious transitions like *first, second,* and *third,* there are other ways to move from point to point. Sometimes a brief pause is all you need to indicate that you've finished one subject and are turning to another.

You can use quotes as transition points too, introducing a new subject with the words of someone else. A well-chosen and well-placed anecdote can also help you get smoothly on your way.

In general, though, good transitions are like good openings: they are often written after the speech exists.

71

If they don't come naturally to you, write the entire speech, then go back and strengthen your transitions.

TELL THEM WHAT YOU TOLD THEM: WAYS TO CLOSE

It's important to remind your audience of what you've said when you reach the end of your speech. This is your chance to sum it all up, memorably, and send them off with something to think about.

Think of your speech as a circle, with the close coming around to connect again with the opening.

If you used a quotation to start, refer to it as you end.

> *All wars are not among thieves. Some are fought by honorable people, for honorable purposes.*

If you began with a question, restate it and provide the answer.

> *Does a good president have to have military experience? Judging from the example set by Lincoln, Wilson, and Franklin Roosevelt . . . the answer is clearly no.*

If you told an anecdote, recall the characters and tell how things turned out for them, or how they might have turned out differently had your plan been adopted.

> *And without mandatory drug testing, innocent students like Melissa Jones would not have suffered needlessly.*

If you began with a joke, repeat the punch line—with a twist. For instance, the speaker who began by quoting the hotel sign, "Please leave your values at the front desk," ended the speech:

72

Clearly, as a company, we have not left our values at the desk.

If you started off with shocking facts, tell how the action you propose could alter those statistics.

If alcohol companies could be compelled to change their tactics and to stop appealing to young people in their ads, teenagers would drink less, their overall health would improve, and violent crimes would decrease.

If you opened by challenging the audience's assumptions, conclude by affirming the new ideas you introduced.

Schools are no worse than they were fifty years ago, and students are not dumber. But the challenges of living and working in a competitive global economy are intense, and we will have to change our education policy if we expect today's students to be successful in tomorrow's jobs.

Other Ways to Close

There's no law that says you can't use a different kind of ending. But whatever technique you use, make sure your finish is strong. It will be the last thing your audience hears, and the words they are most likely to remember.

Use a quote to introduce your final paragraph, or to conclude it. Choose one that summarizes your ideas, that sounds conclusive.

Actress Ruth Gordon said, Never face facts, but we must face them, and the facts are these. . . .

*At an outdoor rally, this speaker's
ending is a call for action.*

I think you'll agree that the time for selfishness is past. Each of us must put aside some time to serve the country, whether in the Armed Forces or in some alternative form of service. As John Kennedy said, "Ask not what your country can do for you; ask what you can do for your country."

Ask for action. If it's appropriate to your topic, use your close to ask the audience to act.

Now is the time to tell our school board how we feel about drug testing. At tomorrow's meeting, speak out against these procedures. Speak out in favor of freedom.

Finish with an anecdote. Any story you use to close should bring together the main points of your speech. Find or create one that's appropriate.

They say that, after Albert Einstein left Germany, a hundred Nazi professors published a book condemning his theory of relativity. But this didn't bother Einstein. "If I were really wrong," he said, "one professor would have been enough."

Go out with optimism. Tell your audience why you think things are getting better, or why there will be peace, or why you expect sales to rise.

Female athletes will not stop until all professional doors are open. Now, there's finally a woman on the Harlem Globetrotters. It's only a matter of time until there's a woman wearing Yankee pinstripes.

Close with a question. A strong rhetorical question—that is, a question to which you don't expect an answer—can make an effective ending to a speech.

If professional baseball players, many of whom are known offenders, can refuse drug testing, should we as innocent students be tested against our will?

Female athletes can be as swift, and as skilled as their male counterparts. Why should they be denied, on the basis of gender alone, the challenges and rewards of playing professional ball?

Once you have written a complete draft of your speech, put it aside for a time and read, or reread, chapter 6.

SIX

WORKING FROM FIRST DRAFT

In composing, as a general rule, run your pen through every other word you have written; you have no idea what vigor it will give your style.

—Samuel Johnson

Now that the first draft of your speech is complete, you are ready to begin the process of revision. No matter how tempted you are to skip this step, *don't*. Your first draft may contain all your best ideas about your subject, but revising it will make those ideas more easily available to your audience. Never deliver the first draft of a speech.

Revise means "to see again." It implies that you have seen your draft once, you have stopped seeing it, and you have gone back to look at it afresh.

Of course, the "stop seeing it" part isn't always easy to arrange, especially if you are working on short deadlines or if you've left preparation until the last minute. But try to allow at least a night's sleep to intervene between finishing the first draft and beginning the revision process. If this is not possible, give yourself a few hours of a different kind of activity. It's best to do something that does not involve words: go for a run or listen to music. It's also helpful to keep in mind that revision usually takes longer than you think it will or should.

FINDING THE "BONES"

If you've worked from an outline, now's the time to sit down with the outline and your first draft. Compare what you've written with what you planned to say. Did you arrive at the place you hoped to reach? Or did you detour into other topics?

If you strayed from your writing outline, how interesting are your digressions? Should they stay in your speech, or be cut from it? Consider these questions carefully. Often, what began as a tangent can become the backbone and focus of a subsequent draft. You may have wandered into territory so interesting and original that you will decide to follow your head and reshape your speech.

If you didn't write from an outline, now's the time to go through your pages of writing and decide what your key points are. Usually, a speech can handle only three main points that support your basic idea. If you have trouble locating the three main points in your first draft, put the draft aside and start with a fresh piece of paper. One surefire way to get focused on main points is to ask yourself: "If, as I began to speak, I was told that the hall was on fire, what three things would I yell to the audience as I ran out the door?" When you write these things down, you will have the key points of your speech.

Sometimes, the key ideas are clear but a first draft shows they are in the wrong order. Scissors and tape or a glue stick can be helpful. Simply cut up your draft and rearrange it until it makes more sense. Sometimes you'll move sentences; other times whole paragraphs or pages might migrate. Of course, if you are working on a word processor, you can move whole blocks of text without retyping and easily print out a clean copy of your speech.

CUTTING

Cutting is an important step. By its nature, writing is an imprecise process. We tend to use excess language as "scaffolding," as support for what we really mean to set down on paper.

Once the meaning is out, though, and the "house" of the speech is erected, the scaffolding must come down. That's what cutting is for. No doubt you needed those extra words, clauses, sentences, paragraphs, and pages while you were writing, or they would not be there. But your audience doesn't need to hear how you arrived at your statement; it should hear only the statement itself. The more clear, succinct, simple, direct, and compelling you can make that statement during revision, the more easily your audience will hear, appreciate, absorb, and react to it. So get your red or blue pencil ready and cut out everything you don't really need.

First, go through every sentence of your draft and cut unnecessary words. Some are easy to spot: *really, very, sort of, kind of,* and so on. Look, too, for the weasel words—words that soften your meaning or make it less than clear. These include *try* (as in the sentence, "We are going to try to do something about it"), *might, could,* and others. Sometimes, of course, you *will* want to soften your meaning. But in general, use simple, direct statements. They'll sound stronger, and you'll be perceived as a more powerful thinker and speaker.

Loose adjectives, words like *nice* and *pretty,* are another group of words to get rid of altogether. If cutting them out leaves a gaping hole, find a sharper adjective: do you mean *striking, smashing,* or *lovely* instead of nice? A thesaurus (a book of synonyms) is helpful here, but don't get carried away.

In speaking, use words that the ear can hear easily. This means you should avoid words you can't pronounce, which might be anything from *indefinable* to *embouchure*; words that sound like other words (such as *write* and *right*); and words that are too fancy for the surrounding language. A word like *effulgent,* for example, will probably be appropriate only once in a lifetime. In most cases, *bright* will do.

After you've cut the extra words, look for phrases or clauses you don't need such as *of course,* and *needless to say.* Then consider cutting whole sentences. Have you said the same thing twice, in different ways, in separate sentences? Try your speech with one, then the other sentence. Does either work better, or do you need to combine the best parts of each to create a new sentence that says exactly what you mean?

DOES IT MAKE SENSE?

Now that you have cut out all excess, go through the speech again and make notes in the margin next to each paragraph. State the point of each paragraph in a few words. Then reread just these summaries in order, and ask yourself:

1. Do my ideas flow and develop logically?
2. Does my speech add up?
3. Have I left anything out? (If so, write and insert any material you think you need.)

Ask yourself also whether your transitions work well. Have you provided your listeners with guideposts they can hear? Use words like *first, second,* and *third,* when you are making three points, or words like *to begin, next,* and *finally.* These guideposts help your audience know where you are in your speech. Smooth out these and all other connections.

Check, too, to be sure that your assertions are supported by facts. If you've claimed that liquor industry advertising is designed to appeal to teenagers, what evidence did you offer? If you said you thought women would make great major-league ballplayers, what reasons—supported by what evidence—have you put forth? Facts, not platitudes, are what people grab on to and remember. Make sure you've provided enough facts so that your audience will be convinced that what you assert is actually true.

By now you probably think you are through. You have examined words, phrases, clauses, sentences, and paragraphs, and tested each one against the questions: Do I need it? Does it add to my listeners' understanding of my main point, or does it confuse the issue? And you have considered whether or not you have enough factual support for your main points.

But there is one final thing to look for. Is there a phrase, a sentence, a paragraph, a page, that you just love? Some piece of language that stands out as your best work, your favorite part? Trust Samuel Johnson, who said, "Read over your compositions, and, when you meet a passage which you think is particularly fine, strike it out."

Not that it isn't good writing; it probably is. But if it stands out that much, it may not belong in your speech. It may find a home in another speech; it may become a poem, a short story, a letter to your aunt. But take it out of the speech.

WRITING FOR THE EAR

Now that you have cut out all the flab, gotten rid of the scaffolding, checked your transitions, your facts, and the flow of your ideas, take a look, or rather a listen, to what's left.

Read your speech out loud. To yourself. Alone. You

don't need a tape recorder for this. Just pay attention to the way you feel when you read your speech through.

Do the words flow easily, or do you get stuck as words pile up together? Are there too many *s* sounds, so that you feel like a hissing snake as you speak? Or do the words thump along, with no musical rhythm? Have you taken out too many transitional phrases, so that you now need to smooth the listener's way from one idea or sentence to another? Make whatever changes you must so that the speech reads easily and fits your voice.

Think, too, of simplifying your language so that your audience can get your meaning as they hear your words. There is a big difference between the printed page and the spoken word. Readers who get lost in an article can look back to an idea they've read moments before and remind themselves of the flow. But listeners must deal with words spoken into the air that move past inexorably. Your audience will not be able to go back and listen again to what you just said if they didn't understand it the first time. And if they lose the flow of your ideas, they are likely to become bored and restless.

Make your speech so easy to follow and so clear, that your audience will recall point A when you get to point C.

Here are some suggestions you might consider:

1. Use short, simple words rather than long, complex ones.

ORIGINAL	REVISION
initiate	start
exemplify	show
utilize	use
reprimand	scold
conflagration	fire

In progressing from an early career
as a pediatrician to United States
Surgeon General, Dr. Joycelyn Elders has
moved from providing medical care to a
wide range of new responsibilities—
including frequent public addresses.

2. Use parallel construction.
   Original: He came, he saw, and the city was conquered.

   Revision: He came, he saw, he conquered.

3. Group your ideas in threes. For some reason, the ear readily hears words, phrases, and clauses that appear in groups of three.

Whether it's baseball, basketball, or ballet, get some exercise daily.

". . . of the people, by the people, for the people."

It's up to parents, students, and teachers to stop this blatant abuse of justice.

4. Pair elements you wish to compare or contrast.

"Ask not what your country can do for you; ask what you can do for your country."

On the one hand, allowing women to play in the major leagues sounds shocking; on the other hand, it makes sense.

Either colored pencils or marking pens can be used to give your finished sketch more color.

5. Use short, simple sentences for emphasis.

I wish I could tell you there is an easy cure. I can't. There isn't.

6. Repeat key words or phrases you wish to emphasize.

Perennials are beautiful. Perennials are hardy. Perennials are easy to maintain. Why not begin planning your own perennial garden now?

7. Repeat sounds to create interest and link your thoughts. Notice the repeated use of *un* in the example.

Drug testing is unfair. Drug testing is un-American. And drug testing is unreliable.

FITTING INTO YOUR TIME LIMIT

When you picked your topic, you scaled it to your time limit. But now that you have read your speech aloud and timed it, you find that your draft is either too long or too short. What to do?

First, respect the time limit. There's rarely an excuse for speaking much less or much longer than expected, although a minute or two either way probably won't matter. If your speech is too short, you may be tempted to invoke the example of Abraham Lincoln and the Gettysburg Address, which is reported to have been so short most people hadn't really started listening before it was done.

Lincoln's masterpiece is a model of oratory; your situation may not be so fortunate. Maybe the marching band is getting into position or someone is changing costumes or pouring coffee during the time allotted for your speech. Or perhaps your teacher has specified a fifteen-minute speech and will grade you down—no matter how excellent your presentation—if you don't follow instructions to the letter.

Whatever the case, here are some strategies for working with your draft until it fits the space of time you've got to fill.

How to Shorten a Speech

Suppose you've already cut every extra word, clause, phrase, sentence, and paragraph and removed pages of excess, but your speech is still too long. Cheer up: you can still cut more.

Now you are going to remove more than the words that make your ideas cloudy; you are going to remove or simplify some of the ideas themselves.

If you prepared an outline, go back over it and see what you can afford to give up. Be prepared to find some psychic resistance to giving up anything, but be firm with yourself. Something has to go.

Usually, some minor point can be disposed of without doing real damage to the speech. You may have given four reasons why drug testing is a bad idea; perhaps you can manage with three or combine two into one. If you've quoted four facts to prove a point, maybe the strongest two will do. Or maybe an idea you've spent an entire paragraph developing can be treated in a single sentence, or made into a phrase that fits inside another sentence. Be careful when doing this kind of telescoping. Don't let the language and structure become convoluted and hard to hear.

Be prepared to give up some of your subtlety or complexity. It is better to say a few things clearly and well than to say everything you know about a subject and have nothing remembered.

How to Lengthen a Speech

Suppose you've taken out all the excess language, cleared up all fuzziness of thought, and you find yourself with a speech that's short of what's required—whether by three or four minutes, or more.

You may be tempted to put the padding back in, a *really* here, a *very* there, to add a few extra adjectives or an adverb collection. You may be tempted to say the same thing twice.

Don't. There are better ways to lengthen a speech. The trick is to add new information and fresh thought, not just words:

• *Elaborate.* Look back over your draft. Are there places where you can explain in more detail just what you're talking about? For example, if you've said "There are nine players on a baseball team," you could then list the positions. You could say that only nine team members are fielded during the game but that the team is actually a much larger entity, and list all the people, including the owners, the manager, coaches, and so on, who compose the team. The important thing is to add more than just words: add information that is interesting and useful to the audience.

• *Add quotes.* A relevant quote or two can liven up a speech while you lengthen it. Consult a source such as *Peter's Quotations,* and read around in a few topic areas. For instance, in your speech about drug testing, you might consult "education," "force," "freedom and liberty," or "youth." You might find just the quote that will give you a stronger opening or a bridge into the main body of your speech, a quote that raises an issue you haven't thought of before and would like to address, a quote that will help you close your speech in an extra paragraph or two, sending the audience off with something pithy to think about.

• *Insert anecdotes.* Find or create a story to drive home one of your points. In a speech about the importance of brand names, one writer created several fictitious computer companies to help make her point:

You go into a local computer store and say, "I'm in the market for a notebook computer." And the salesman shows you a Widget 180, a personal-size Wing Ding, and a compact Numbercruncher Deluxe.

Now, you've been hearing a lot about IBM and its new lower-priced notebooks. Depending on the kind of person you are, you may or may not ask to see an IBM. But you will certainly wonder why the salesman isn't showing you one. Everyone who thinks computer puts IBM in the top ten—except this guy. Maybe he makes a bigger commission on the Widget 180, you think, or maybe he's unloading Numbercrunchers because the company is going under. Or maybe he just doesn't know his business. You decide to shop elsewhere, just in case.

• *Come up with a new angle.* Try to imagine how some character in history would respond to your speech: "Give me liberty or give me death"?

How would someone from another country respond? "In Russia, we would send you to Siberia for even thinking about using drugs."

How would your mother respond? Or an alien from outer space? Answers to questions like these can often give you additional ideas.

• *Imagine objections to what you've written.* Either think them up on your own, or read your speech to a friend or parent and ask that person to pick holes in your argument. That friendly critic may be able to come up with some objections you haven't considered. Build these into your speech, along with your responses to them, of course, and your speech will not only be longer, it will be stronger too.

Nelson Mandela became an effective public speaker, delivering speeches to audiences around the world to gain support for the South African freedom struggle.

ADDITIONAL REMEDIES

You've cut the fluff. You've made your speech easy to read and easy to listen to. It fits your time limit to the second. But there's still something wrong with it. What then?

Overcoming Dullness

If your speech is dull, underline the sections that you find most interesting. How are they different from the parts you consider dull? What can you do to improve the less interesting parts, bringing them up to the level of the best?

Try making the language more colorful and specific. Use vivid nouns and active verbs. Give clear examples instead of generalities. Adding quotes, statistics, and facts will bring abstractions to life.

> *Original: The kind of exercise you do is less important than how often you do it.*

> *Revision: Pick basketball, or badminton, or ballet. But whatever form of exercise you choose, do it regularly—for at least thirty minutes each session, three times a week.*

Tinker with rhythms and sentence structure. Use sound patterns, like the three *b* words in the example above, to enliven the writing for your listeners.

One word of caution: your speech may be less dull than you think it is. Maybe you've worked on it too long and too hard, to the point where you can't tell what's interesting and what's not. It's happened to others. Ruth Bader Ginsburg, now a Supreme Court justice, once gave a speech on *Roe* v. *Wade* that she thought was boring. The speech ignited a battle among feminists that isn't over yet. So, before you decide it's really dull, ask an honest and compassionate friend's opinion.

Combatting Oversimplicity

What if your speech sounds too simple? Albert Einstein used to say that a thing should be as simple as possible, but no simpler. Simple can be good. Just don't confuse simple with stupid. True simplicity, and the clarity that goes with it, are very difficult to achieve and worth struggling for. Don't succumb to the temptation to make things sound more complex than they are.

But if you think your speech really does sound too simple, perhaps it's your sentence structure. Do most of your sentences follow the subject-verb-object pattern? Introduce a little variety.

If sentence structure isn't the problem, work on using more colorful and specific language.

Combatting Complication

If your speech is too complicated, go back to step 1 of the speech-writing process. Ask yourself, What one thing am I trying to say? Make sure every sentence and paragraph adds something and helps convey the main thought. Simplify sentence structure. Use easier words.

After each difficult sentence, ask yourself: What do I mean? How can I say this in other words? Write those other words down, or have someone take notes as you say them, or record them into a tape recorder and transcribe them. Those other words probably say, simply and exactly, just what you want your audience to know.

If your speech is full of complicated information, though, you may want to consider using visual aids to help your audience grasp in one quick look what words can never fully explain.

USING VISUAL AIDS

*A picture shows me at a glance what it takes
dozens of pages of a book to expound.*

—Ivan Turgenev

Everyone knows a picture is worth at least a thousand words. That probably explains why most business and professional speakers use visual aids such as slides to accompany their speeches.

The slides they use might include charts and graphs that show the growth of sales in dollars and units, or this year's profits versus last year's, or how many widgets the U.S. Widget Company has to manufacture to break even.

Word slides are also popular. You might see "Sell, Sell, Sell," in increasingly large letters, highlighted with neon and rainbow effects. A slide could show a list of the magazines where the company's newest ads will run, or the four steps store managers can take to stop shoplifting, or ten ways to eliminate waste.

Sometimes the slides show pictures: faces of target customers, shots of ads used in the new campaign, or magazine covers arranged in a graceful fan. Pictures of new products, manufacturing facilities, even political or satirical cartoons might appear on slides that accompany a speech.

Unless you are speaking about your trip to Greece or giving a talk on a subject such as art history or architecture, for which premade slides are readily available, slides such as those used by professional and business speakers will probably be out of the question.

But visual aids can still be adapted to your needs as a speaker. Simpler technologies, including flip charts, blackboards, and overhead projectors, can help you add visual interest when it's your turn at the podium. And newer technologies, including computer generated graphics and video, can help put your points across, too.

DO YOU NEED VISUALS?

Before you decide how you wish to present your graphics to an audience, however, determine whether they will add anything to your speech. Read through your revised text, looking for places where a picture would be appropriate. Some occasions are obviously inappropriate for visuals. You probably wouldn't use a flip chart if you were delivering a valedictory address on the value of being true to yourself. On the other hand, some topics cry out for illustration. Travel, fine art, gardening—all highly visual subjects—may be hard to address without the help of pictures.

Are there spots where you use a great many words to explain a statistic that could easily be illustrated? Are you presenting many statistics which when read aloud are hard to relate to each other but when pictured become immediately clear?

Are any of your quotes from sources that were originally visual, such as captions from cartoons? Does it take many words to explain the visual, and then is the impact lost?

A Book Versus a Potato

Visuals can become the subject of controversy. When the vice presidential debates in the U.S. election campaign of 1992 were being planned, Vice President Dan Quayle argued that he should be allowed to bring to the debate a copy of Democratic candidate Al Gore's book about the environment. Gore's team didn't want Quayle quoting from the book onstage, so they countered that Quayle could bring the book if Gore could bring a potato. Since Dan Quayle had recently embarrassed himself by publicly misspelling the word *potato*, this was an unacceptable compromise. No visual aids were used.

Is there any person, place, or thing that must be shown for the audience to understand your subject?

Would illustrations make understanding easier, or would they just be window dressing, nice but not really necessary?

Adding visuals to a dull or poorly written speech will not improve it, and no one will be fooled. Words are the basic building blocks of speeches, and words come first. Only when words prove inadequate because of the nature of the subject—not the ability of the writer—should pictures be called on to help.

If you decide you need pictures to go with some of your words, don't sprinkle your illustrations throughout the speech. Instead, isolate them into a single area: you might include charts of statistics showing the rise of alcohol and drug use among teenagers at the beginning of your speech. Your audience will still be fresh enough to absorb them, and once your facts are established you can leave the visuals behind and go on to

*With the assigned task of explaining
the Heimlich technique of assistance to
a choking person, this speaker used a
volunteer as a visual aid.*

your arguments and conclusions. Or you may decide to videotape or photograph alcohol advertisements aimed at teenagers and use them for evidence for a section of your speech.

Sometimes, just thinking about adding visuals to a speech can help tighten an already good draft. It's an exercise worth doing. For each paragraph, write a word or phrase that you want your audience to remember, and draw an appropriate illustration. For example:

- Teenage drug usage on the rise—chart
- Response of law enforcement agencies—photo of law officers
- Why drug testing in high schools won't work—four reasons
- What parents can do to discourage drug use—three steps

After you've done this for the speech, consider whether you really need the pictures or whether you can create the picture with language. For instance, talk about the dramatic rise of drug usage, rather than using a chart. Create a word picture of drug arrest procedures. State that there are four reasons why drug testing won't work, and introduce each with *first, second, third,* and *fourth.* Do the same with the three steps to discourage drug use.

There are two more points to consider. First, if your speech is for the classroom, check with your teacher that it's OK to use visual aids. Second, make sure the equipment you need will be available. Don't assume there will be a blackboard or an easel or an overhead projector. Plan ahead. Ask.

VISUAL AIDS TO CONSIDER

Suppose you have read through your speech, marked and grouped all the potential visuals, and decided that you do need or want to illustrate some of your material. What kinds of help are available?

Blackboards

Good teachers know the value of this simple tool. Blackboards are widely available, fun, and easy to use. They are inexpensive and effective.

When using a blackboard, write only the most important words. Remember, you want to emphasize key points. Plan what you will write ahead of time, working it out on paper if need be.

Be sure to write legibly. Better yet, print. Write large, using your whole arm. Press firmly on the chalk.

You can write more than words on a blackboard. Drawings and diagrams can be very helpful. When talking about a football play, the history of an idea, or the logic of a computer program, you can use the blackboard to help make your points.

Flip Charts

If you like the idea of a blackboard but one isn't available, you can use a flip chart to much the same effect. You will need a pad of large paper, at least 14 by 17 inches, an easel to stand it on, and some broad-tipped markers.

The key item in this list is the easel. You can't hold a large pad of paper and draw and talk at the same time. And there's no satisfactory substitute for an easel. Makeshift propping will end with your visual on the floor and you in a frenzy. If you can't get an easel, use a different visual format or none at all.

You can use a flip chart in three ways: preprinted, prepared, or written on the spot:

1. *Preprinted* means just that: you draw your charts, graphs, maps, or write out your key words and phrases on the pages before you speak. The pages then become the notes you

use to speak from. If you are comfortable ad-libbing, with only charts and graphs to remind you of your key points, this can be an effective form of speaking.

2. You could also prepare your flip charts ahead of time. But this time, instead of using dark markers, you write out your points and sketch in your charts lightly with pencil. While you are speaking you simply go over the light writing with a marker. Your words and diagrams become visible to the audience: it appears as if you are creating the charts as you go.

While this method is safe, it can also be dull. Be careful not to look as if you are writing over something that's already there; you must practice using your marker as if your thoughts are flowing as your arm is moving.

3. The third way of using a flip chart, writing on it as you speak, assures spontaneity. Speakers who create flip charts as they go along seem—and usually are—exceptionally confident and in control. They have good memories; they don't forget what they meant to write or draw mid-speech. However, if you're shaky about your memory, it's best to prepare your flip charts ahead of time.

Overhead Projectors

Overhead projectors are available in many schools and businesses. The information to be presented is printed on a plastic sheet, or transparency, which is laid on a glass plate on the projector. A light shines through the transparency, and the image it contains is magnified through an overhead glass and projected on a screen in the front of the room.

While overhead projectors can be effective tools, remember that transparencies must be prepared ahead of time. You can do this either by writing on them with a grease pencil or having them prepared from typed documents through your school's audiovisual department. Or you can print them yourself, if you have a suitable graphics or word-processing program and a laser printer at your disposal.

Remember that overhead projectors, like slides, are usually used in darkened rooms. For many people, darkness equals sleep. It's easier to lose your audience's attention when the lights are low. If you use an overhead be sure both you and your visuals are compelling.

Show and Tell: The Power of Props

Sometimes the best visual is the thing itself. If you're discussing an article in *Time* magazine, bring in the issue and quote from it. If you're talking about how shoes are made, you might point to parts of an actual shoe as you detail each process.

There are lots of possibilities, as long as you feel comfortable going a little bit show business. One speaker, for instance, addressing a group of overworked social workers, told them they needed a new uniform, and then pulled a Superman costume out of a suitcase. Another business speaker arrived onstage riding a bicycle, to demonstrate that movement is necessary to maintain balance.

The show-and-tell technique works best with a small audience in a fairly small room, where it's possible for everyone to clearly see the object you are holding up. Better yet, if the item is small enough, pass it around. If the exhibit isn't large enough to be seen when you hold it up to discuss it, read from it, or use it as a prop, then don't bring it.

MAKING INFORMATION VISUAL

Now that you have selected your medium, decide how you will put your information into visual form.

Words

Whether you're using a blackboard, a flip chart, or overheads, you can use words as visuals to make your points and help your audience remember them. Use as few words as possible, and make sure they are hard-hitting, expressing your thought concisely in a memorable way.

If you are making a list, use parallel construction and the same size lettering for items of similar importance.

For example, suppose you want to use words to emphasize the three main reasons why you feel drug testing of students by the school board would be unfair. The two models below show the right and wrong ways to present the list:

DRUG TESTING IS UNFAIR BECAUSE

- All students are equally suspect.
- Test results are not accurate.
- Constitutional rights are violated.

Drug testing is unfair because
- ALL STUDENTS ARE EQUALLY SUSPECT.
- INACCURATE results.
- VIOLATION OF rights.

The lettering style is inconsistent in the second example and the arguments are not presented in a parallel fashion.

Maps

Whether you are describing your trip through Italy, detailing Washington's march on Trenton, or showing the size of the United States before and after the Louisiana Purchase, a map can help. In fact, when you need a map, nothing else will really do.

Unfortunately, most maps aren't big enough to be

100

read from more than a foot away. Others are too big to hold. Tack a map to a wall if the map is big enough for your audience to see. Or draw a map on the black-board, or on a flip chart or overhead transparency. These sketches will be rough but can demonstrate the geography of a country, or the movement of various forces, or the distance from a city to the sea.

Charts and Graphs

Numerical information that is muddled by language can be easily understood when you use a chart or graph. Consider these examples:

Words without chart

> *Now I'd like to talk about our sales in relation to profits for 1993 versus 1992. In 1992, we sold 4.2 million widgets and made a profit of $1,260,000. In 1993, we sold 4.5 million widgets, but our profit was only $1,240,000. Obviously, our sales-to-profit ratio has declined. We are making only a 27.5 percent profit in 1993, whereas we made 30 percent in 1992. We are selling more widgets but making less money.*

Words with chart

	1992	*1993*
Sales units	4.2 million	4.5 million
Profits	$1.26 million	$1.24 million
Sales/Profit ratio	30.0 percent	27.5 percent

> *As you can see, though our sales have increased slightly during the past year, our profits have declined. We are selling more widgets, but making less money.*

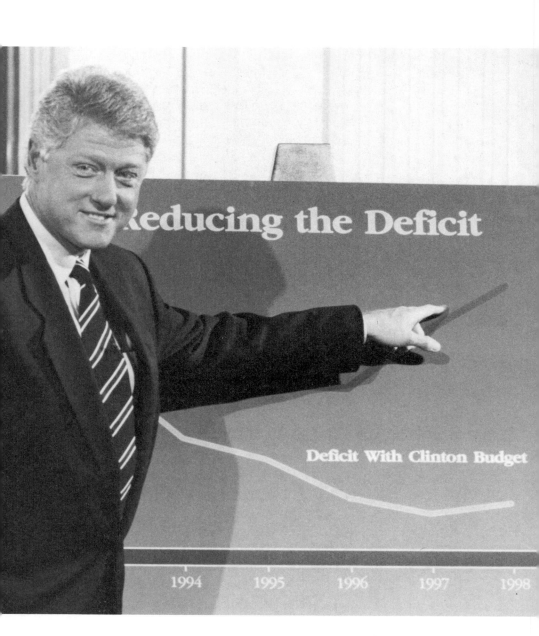

Reducing the Deficit

Deficit With Clinton Budget

1994   1995   1996   1997   1998

In an address to the public, President
Bill Clinton used a chart to explain a
plan to reduce the federal deficit.

Even the simplest chart can help you to eliminate some fairly confusing language while it enables you to present information clearly and concisely. Many charts and graphs are easy to do and can be drawn with ease on the board, on a flip chart, or on a transparency. Here are some of the most useful kinds:

1. *Tables.* The chart above is actually a table: a short, neatly arranged list of various items, as in a table of contents.

Keep tables simple. Don't try to include too much. In the example above, for instance, you might include one more line (perhaps sales in dollars) or one more column (another year's actual or projected results). More than that and the table would be too cluttered to be useful.

Also be sure your numbers line up. Keep decimal points under one another. If you are adding or subtracting numbers in a column or row, be sure your math is correct—or someone in the audience is bound to call you on it!

2. *Line Graphs.* Line graphs are classics. You've seen them tacked to the back wall in many business cartoons. They feature jagged lines that shoot up and fall down, creating peaks and valleys. Some dips and rises are steeper than others.

Line graphs are excellent for showing changes in quantity over time: changes in sales, profits, production, whatever. The bottom axis, the horizontal, always indicates time. You may divide it up as you like: by days, months, years, even centuries. Just be certain you use the same unit of time all the way across and that the divisions are equal.

The vertical axis, on the left-hand side, is used to indicate quantities. Again, be sure increments are even, and do not include more information than your audience can handle. At most, graph three quantities on the same line graph. If you need to show more, use a separate graph. The point is to make the information clear, not to jam as much onto one visual as possible.

3. *Bar Charts*. Bar charts are useful for comparing quantities. You might use a bar chart to show how many cars were sold versus how many trucks, year by year, for several years. The bars can be horizontal or vertical.

Again, don't put too much information on a single chart. Your audience needs only a snapshot of the relationship of one quantity to another, not a documentary. Keep it simple.

Pictures

If you can get good, large-size photos of what you wish to illustrate, by all means use them. You need something that can be seen from a distance. Oversize glossy magazines are good sources for photos showing the results of plastic surgery, the effect of a hurricane, the size of a crowd gathered to greet a hero, and so on.

Videotapes

Many business and professional speakers use video clips—one- to three-minute segments of videotape—to illustrate their points or present information. If video playback equipment will be available, you can show a short segment of videotape as part of your speech.

Visibility is important. A regular home-sized video screen will probably be clearly seen by only about twenty people. Larger screens and projection devices make video visible much further away.

Once you solve the visibility issue, you might choose to show clips of alcohol commercials that are aimed at teenagers, for example, in a speech about drug use, or some slow-motion footage of three major-league hitters for a talk on batting styles.

Video rental stores, public libraries, and materials

taped on your home recorder are all potential sources of footage. Or, if you own or can rent a video camera, you might want to create some video footage to support your talk.

Whatever your source, be sure to introduce your video clip and to provide transitions away from it. Let your audience know what they are about to see.

Now I'm going to show you a brief videotape of X, Y, and Z at the plate.

And be sure to let them know how the tape relates to what you are talking about.

You'll see a variety of stances here, illustrating my point that there's more than one way to swing a bat.

After the tape, connect back to your topic.

I think you'll agree that many of today's beer commercials make a blatant appeal to teens.

Remember, speeches are made of words—spoken words, not images. None of the techniques for enlivening a speech with visuals will make a bad speech good. But a creative and correct use of visuals can be like the salt on the potato chips: that little something that adds a lot. Visuals can help your audience both understand and remember your message better. They can make the difference between OK and excellent.

EIGHT

PRACTICING YOUR DELIVERY

Diamonds are only chunks of coal that stuck to their jobs.

—Minnie Richard Smith

If you've polished your speech, you might think it's already a diamond. But no matter how well written your draft, it's at best only a diamond in the rough. Until your voice makes the words and phrases live, it's not a speech. And your delivery will to a large extent determine how your audience listens, and whether or not they actually hear what you have to say.

Even if you've gone over your speech a hundred times, it's new when you stand before the audience, because the situation is different. There's an extra lift of adrenaline, the exciting edge you get from being on. If you've practiced well, you'll be able to use that energy. If you haven't, that surge of adrenaline may overwhelm you. Decide to practice.

It might help to think of your speech as a baseball and to imagine the perfect pitch. It's on time and on target. It does exactly what the pitcher wants it to do. Whether it's high, wide, inside, fast, or slow, it's under control.

You'll want that kind of command over your delivery. You'll want to be able to slow down, speed up, emphasize forcefully or soften what you're saying with a gesture. To get that level of major-league command, you'll need practice.

How much practice? Lots. One successful corporate executive who speaks regularly says a new speech requires ten times as long to practice as to give. That means for every half hour of speaking, she will spend five hours practicing.

Now, she's a perfectionist. To be an excellent speaker, you may need less practice than that. Assume you will need at least three times as long as you will speak, and the more, the better—up to a limit of ten times the length of your speech.

Can you practice too much? Some people say yes. Rehearsing a thousand times before your performance could take all the fun out of it. On the other hand, not enough practice could lead to a bad case of stage fright and no rehearsal skills to fall back on. Actually, few people ever practice their delivery to the point where it results in a dull performance.

This chapter contains hints for practicing and delivering your text. You probably won't use them all. Instead, choose the ones that appeal to you and give them a try.

First, though, prepare the materials you will use when you stand up to speak. What you need depends on whether you will read your speech, speak from note cards, or work from memory.

PREPARING YOUR TEXT

Reading from a prepared text, either typed pages or a teleprompter, is preferred by business speakers and politicians. The text provides a clear set of things to say. The pressure is taken off remembering, and the speaker's emphasis and energy can be spent on the delivery.

If you decide to read your speech, type it double- or triple-spaced. Use wide margins, at least an inch on the right- and left-hand sides. You might type each sentence as a separate paragraph (See Figure 1). Indent the first word at least five spaces from the left margin and leave an extra space between each sentence.

Making each sentence a separate paragraph lets you see how long each sentence is. Shorten those that look too long—any that run more than four or five lines. Ideally, each sentence should run no more than two or three typed lines. Some could be only a single line.

The space between the paragraph/sentences gives you room to pause, and breathe. It also allows time for the audience to take in what you've said. Ideally, it should allow them time to agree with you.

Use capitals and lowercase letters when you type your speech, rather than all capitals. This makes it easier for your eye to know when a sentence begins. If you have access to a typewriter with a large typeface such as Orator, by all means use it.

If you can use a word-processing program and a printer that allows you to print your text in different fonts, take advantage of technology. Many professional speakers prepare their texts in Helvetica or Garamond typefaces, in font sizes ranging from 14 to 18 points (See Figure 2). Try printing out a page or two of your text in different fonts and see which is easiest for you to read.

It's a good idea to spell out everything just as you will say it. Write out "twenty-one" and "Equal Rights Amendment," rather than using the numerals 21 and the abbreviation ERA. Again, the point is to make it

Figure 1: Type your speech with each sentence appearing as a separate paragraph.

Thank you, Hal ... and good morning.

It's a pleasure to be with you again this year.

My peers have already talked with you about what our company is doing to bring you computers with improved speed, additional function, and lower prices.

I want to focus on skill—or rather, on skills—this morning . . . and the role they play in our ability to compete successfully . . . as a company, and also as a country . . . in the global economy.

I was in a session a couple of weeks ago with Walter Wristen, a man whom many credit with the transformation of the banking industry in the '70s.

He delivered a speech to the Royal Society of Arts in Manufacturing entitled ''The Twilight of Sovereignty.''

He pointed out that we stand at a watershed in history . . .

Information technology has already demolished time and distance . . . and Wristen proposes that technology has been the greatest driver in the incredible changes we have seen in national sovereignty.

It is clearly changing the way we work, the nature of the work we do, and the kinds of skills we require.

Good morning.

It's a pleasure to be with you today, to talk about the revolutions that are under way in technology, in our customers' businesses, and at IBM—as well, as about the role education and training can play in these transformations.

I've noticed that it's not unusual for technology and revolution to go hand in hand.

They say that during the French Revolution a visitor from Paris stopped by a small village, and was asked by a friend what was happening in the city.

``Well,'' said the visitor, ``they are using that new invention, the guillotine, and cutting off heads by the thousands.''

``How terrible!'' cried the villager. ``That could ruin my hat business.''

PAUSE

Now, in most cases, technology is good for business.

For instance, it's been said that the Industrial Revolution increased productivity by a factor of about a hundred.

Figure 2:   You can read your speech
from a typed script.

easy—when you are under stress—to say exactly what you mean.

Remove as many stumbling blocks as possible from your script. You will be nervous (even if only slightly). Make your speech simple for the eye.

Finally, number your pages at the top center. Should your speech come apart on your way to the podium, you will be able to put it back together quickly.

PREPARING NOTES OR AN OUTLINE

Speaking from notes or an outline instead of a complete text can be very effective, especially if you are an articulate person who has no trouble finding words or putting them together into coherent sentences. (See Figure 3.)

Build your outline or notes from the draft you've prepared. Go through what you've written and underline the topic sentences. Then number the subsidiary or supporting points. Mark key phrases, spots where the language is precise and important. Unless you are a gifted natural speaker, your written phrases are probably better than those you will think up on the spot. Make sure your best writing makes it to your outline or note cards: you don't want it to go to waste.

Whether you prepare a one- or two-page outline or put your thoughts onto index cards is up to you. Sheets are less likely to scatter across the floor as you advance to the podium. Cards, whether 3 by 5 or 4 by 6, may seem less conspicuous than sheets of paper, and looking through them as you speak will give you something to do with your hands.

Whichever you choose, type or print your outline or notes plainly on one side of the paper or note cards. Make sure that they are easy to read. Leave enough space so that you can add additional points or phrases as they occur to you during practice. Number your pages or cards boldly at the very top.

*With a clear, well-prepared outline
in hand, this speaker is at ease.*

```
              PAUSE

Technology good for business.

   -Industrial Revolution increased
productivity 100X

   -Micro-electronic revolution enhanced
productivity 1 million times—and not over

But revolutions make it harder to get things
done

   Changes in

      -markets

      -products

      -methodologies
```

Figure 3:   Or you can deliver the
speech from an outline.

MEMORIZING

Both the prepared text and the cards described above can be useful to the speaker who must memorize.

First, memorize your outline. Think of it as getting the skeleton of your speech in mind. Then memorize the language you need to flesh it out.

Ultimately, your outline may prove more useful to you than the exact words you've written. If you forget a few words, you can always move on to the next point of the outline. If you forget your line of reasoning—the logical development of your argument—even if you remember the words, you can be in real trouble.

113

Unless you are delivering a speech written by someone else, or your teacher is holding a copy of your text and checking your memory against it, only you will know the words you are supposed to say. And only you will know if you miss one or two, or change a phrase here or there in mid-speech.

YOUR VOICE

When your text, outline, or cards are ready, set them aside for a few moments and pay attention to your voice.

How does your throat feel? How does it feel when you think about standing up in front of a group and delivering your speech? How does it feel when you open your mouth and begin to speak?

Chances are when you think about speaking, or when you begin, your throat will feel tight: just a little, or maybe a lot. Yet how relaxed your throat is will influence the quality of your voice: whether it sounds warm and melodious or tight and frightened.

In general, the best thing you can do for your voice and your delivery is to relax. Don't cough or clear your throat. Those actions will only tense your throat muscles further. Instead take a sip of water—not too cold—and swallow it. Inhale deeply, and exhale, mouth open, letting your jaw drop. Pick up your speech, outline, or note cards and begin to speak, pretending you are in front of the group.

Now really listen to yourself. How does your voice sound? If it's controlled, warm, and easy—fine. If you don't like what you hear, check each of the points that follow.

Posture

Are you standing straight? Is your neck straight? It's easier to produce a good sound when you are standing

114

correctly. Even tilting your head to the side slightly or bending forward to look at your notes can put a slight strain on your throat. Don't stand like a general, but do stand tall; straighten your head as you let your shoulders drop.

Breathing

Can you breathe freely? Your voice is produced by air passing through your larynx, or voice box; and the more freely and easily you can breathe, the more easily you will speak. Loosen your collar and tie, remove that choker, and let your belt out a notch or two so you can breathe.

Also, remember that it's difficult to breathe easily just after a big meal. Eat lightly before practicing and especially before the actual performance.

Exercises for Relaxing

Here are some exercises that will help you relax so you can speak more easily.

Yawn, or move your mouth as if you were yawning. Tilt your head back as you do. Feel your throat muscles loosen.

Rotate your head slowly forward, right, back, left, then around the opposite way.

Bend forward from the shoulder and sway loosely—be Raggedy Ann or Andy for a moment. Then stand up straight, breathe deeply, and exhale.

HINTS FOR YOUR PRACTICE PERFORMANCE

Begin reading your speech aloud. This is no time to criticize your writing. Major revisions should be unnecessary at this point; you've revised carefully already. You may need to make minor word changes if you find what you've written is difficult to pronounce or if it sounds odd when you read it. If you're speaking from notes, you may want to jot down a fortuitous phrase that occurs to you during practice so you'll remember it at the podium. You may rearrange phrases for better rhythm, but resist the impulse to do major rewrites. Just read.

Here are some things to pay attention to.

Speed

Many people talk too fast when they get nervous. Others can't get words out at all. Practice reading slowly. And then more slowly. Then a bit faster. Knowing you can control the rate at which you read will help when the first rush of adrenaline hits you at the podium.

Practice varying your speed through the speech to give it texture. Convey your meaning by careful pacing, pausing at commas, breathing at the ends of sentences. You may want to mark significant pauses, or places where you need to take a breath, right in your text.

Emphasis

Emphasize important words, underlining them with your voice, so that your meaning will be clear to your audience. Underline them in your text too, as you practice, so you will remember which words you want to stress. Put the weight of your voice where it will do the most good. A shift in emphasis can reinforce or change meaning. Consider the difference in emphasis subtle shifts can make in this quote from Abraham Lincoln:

> If the *good* people, in *their* wisdom, shall see fit to keep *me* in the background, I have been *too familiar* with disappointments to be very *much* chagrined.
> *If the good people*, in their *wisdom*, shall *see fit* to keep me in the *background*, I have been too familiar with *disappointments* to be very much *chagrined*.

116

The first version places more emphasis on the speaker's distinguishing between "them" (the good people) and "me" (the speaker). The second version places the emphasis—more correctly—on how the speaker will feel if not elected.

OTHER HINTS FOR PRACTICE

If you find yourself gasping for breath, shorten your sentences or mark pauses in your prepared script.

If you are saying "em" and "eh" between words, these verbal tics will interfere with your meaning. Your audience may start paying more attention to these extra sounds than to your message.

Speak clearly. Pronounce all the words. Don't slur over syllables.

Speak loudly. Practice projecting: directing your voice so that it can be heard clearly at a distance.

It may take several readings until you are comfortable with your delivery and have marked your text to indicate where to slow down, speed up, or emphasize. These variations will give life and color to your presentation. You might find it helpful to make notes on an extra copy of your text as you work out the dynamics of your speech. Then you can transfer only the marks you really need to the copy you'll speak from.

After you've marked your speech, read it aloud to yourself two or three times, just to get the sound of it. Then try reading to a mirror. You can practice eye contact and work out gestures. Use your hands and your head and your posture as necessary to reinforce what your words are saying. Lean forward for emphasis. Lift one hand, then the other, as you state opposing sides of an argument.

Using a Practice Audience

When you've finished working with a mirror, read your speech to someone you know—friend, parent, brother, or sister—anyone who will listen. Practice making eye contact, and put in all the emphases, gestures, pacing, and so on, that you've already rehearsed alone.

If you make a mistake, keep going. You want to practice the total speech, not just a portion. Besides, you need to work out what you'll do if you should happen to skip a line or mispronounce a word.

- *Using audience feedback (what they say).* Ask your practice audience what they think of your speech. You hope they will say, "That's the best speech I ever heard. You were wonderful."

  But what if they are critical? Don't be defensive. You want to learn. You want to improve. Listen to what they say. And listen to more than their words. Your audience may not know how to tell you what really needs improvement. But they can usually point to the places that need work. Ask questions, trying to get your listeners to pinpoint just what bothered them, if anything. If Aunt Essie says the beginning was weak, does she mean what you said, or how you said it, or both?

  Have confidence in yourself. Ultimately, you will decide whether to go with the ending as it stands or alter it somewhat because three people said it didn't work for them. Listen to comments patiently, evaluate them calmly, and decide whether they're useful. If they are, make changes. If not, forget them.
- *Using audience feedback (their body language).* Besides what your listeners say, pay attention to their body language as you speak. Are they looking at you attentively? Fidgeting? Nodding and yawning? Try to read the subtle messages they are giving you. Making a speech is a kind of dialogue, but what the audi-

*Audience feedback: fidgeting, yawning,
and talking are clear warning signals.*

ence has to say is usually communicated without words. Learning to "listen" to it will make you a better speaker.

If they are nodding in agreement, you know you're doing well.

If they are yawning, the room may be stuffy or you may not be speaking loudly enough or clearly enough or with enough energy. You may not have enough variety in your pitch or pacing. A singsong monotone will put people to sleep faster than Brahms's Lullaby.

What if the audience seems restless or shuffling? These are signs that they are not engaged. You need to hook up with them again. Are you making eye contact? Are you looking up from the page at all? Try stepping forward, speaking up, animating your gestures.

PRACTICING WITH A TAPE RECORDER OR VIDEO EQUIPMENT

It's always helpful to read to people; they give you instant, emotional feedback, and audience reactions are invaluable.

However, reading into a tape recorder, and especially practicing before a video camera, can help you see yourself as others see you. Be prepared for a shock when you first play back what you've taped: it may not sound or look like you. But the shock wears off quickly if you just keep listening or watching.

Here are some hints for working with audio- and videotape.

Working with a Tape Recorder

Record, then play back, your entire speech. Listen without looking at your text or outline. Follow the ideas. Do they make sense? Are transitions clear? Do the thoughts flow logically? Does your voice shift to accommodate changes in thought and to emphasize im-

How to Read a Speech

Audiences don't like to be read to; they like to be talked to. The difference is largely a matter of eye contact.

When you speak to a friend, you make eye contact as you begin a sentence. Then, you may look away, over your friend's shoulder, say, or around the room, in the middle of your sentence. As you come to the end of the sentence, you look at your friend again.

In contrast, when you read out loud you probably look down at the text at the beginning of each sentence, up at the audience in mid-sentence, then down at the text as the sentence ends.

The trick to making reading look more like talking, then, is to change your normal pattern of looking at the text. Look up at the audience as you begin a sentence. Let your eyes dip to the page and pick up a few more words and phrases as you near the middle of the sentence. Look back up at the audience as it ends.

At first, this style of reading will seem very difficult and artificial. But with practice, you'll quickly improve your presentation and your speaking manner.

portant meanings? Is your voice interesting to listen to, varied and yet controlled? Do your pauses heighten your meaning? Is your speech free of the clutter of "ehs," "ers," and "ums"?

After listening through once, listen again, this time with text in hand. What is the best thing about your reading? How can you get more of that? Are there any changes you should make based on how the speech sounds? Is there anything you can write on the text to help you to do something well or to improve? Make comments on your typescript. You may want to tape the speech again and listen to how you have improved.

Working with Video

If you're lucky enough to know someone who can videotape your practice, you can noticeably improve your delivery in a very short time.

Begin by reading just a page or two of your text into the camera. Then play it back. Check to see that you're not making annoying gestures, such as pushing your glasses up or scratching your head. But more important, notice when your eyes look down at the page. Chances are you look down at the beginning and at the end of every sentence, and up in the middle of the sentence. This is how most people read.

Follow the suggestions for audiotape, just listening, eyes closed, to your delivery. Mark your text as noted above.

Finally, look *and* listen. You'll see and hear how you can improve.

Practicing your delivery—whether with a live audience or on tape—can be fun, and the rewards of preparation can't be overemphasized. You'll find yourself more confident, so even if you make a small error or two, you won't be thrown.

As a final step, if you can arrange it, stage a dress rehearsal in the room where you will speak. That way, you can become familiar with the layout of the room, the setup of the podium, the lights, the acoustics. If you can't arrange this, don't worry: you've worked hard, you're at ease with your speech, you're ready to go.

ᗧELIVERING YOUR SPEECH

It is in performance that the sudden panic hits. . . .
A well-meaning friend says, "There's nothing to be
nervous about," and it almost helps, because the
desire to strangle distracts us for the moment.

—Eloise Ristad

Performance isn't practice. Dress rehearsal isn't opening night. That difference doesn't have to be frightening: it can be the stuff of exhilaration.

Besides, there are techniques that can help minimize the novelty of the situation, so that the energy you feel is something you can use, not something that stops you. Experience is one good way to get comfortable with pre-performance jitters. But there are other ways as well. Some techniques relate directly to speaking, while others focus on feeling good about yourself.

CONSIDER WHAT YOU'LL WEAR

Dress appropriately, not too dressy or too casual. Ask advice if you don't know what's right. Of course, in some cases, you won't have a choice. As valedictorian, you'll probably wear a cap and gown. At a black-tie dinner, you'll be formally dressed. But what about other occasions, such as a speech in class?

Wear something comfortable, something familiar, something you feel good in, rather than brand-new clothes. You will want to breathe freely, so loose is better than tight. Avoid close collars, ties that choke, and constricting necklaces. Clanking jewelry will distract both you and your audience, so leave it home.

In general, dress up a little. It's an honor to be asked to speak, and while it might be corny to say that as you stand up in front of a group, it's fine to say "I'm honored to be here" by the way you're dressed.

Jackets add authority to both men and women. Wear yours over a neatly pressed shirt or blouse with a crisp collar; soft collars such as those on knit polo shirts rumple and look sloppy.

Grooming is important, too. Hair that hangs in your eyes, glasses that slip to the tip of your nose, dingy teeth, and dirty fingernails all say "I don't care about myself—or my audience." And slipshod grooming can distract from what you're going to say.

Don't try a new hairstyle or get a drastic cut the day before you speak—what if you hate it? It's probably best not to experiment too wildly with makeup either. Do what you normally do, so you can feel at ease. The more certain you are that you look good, the less you will have to think about it and the more energy you will be able to focus on your speech.

Now you're perfectly groomed and dressed. But you say you've been up the last three nights watching that late-night comic with the wacky skits? And over the weekend you skied nonstop then crammed all night for a chemistry exam?

Exhausted is the worst thing to be when you have to give a speech. Maybe you remember how awful Bill Clinton looked and sounded as the 1992 presidential campaign wound down. Rest both your body and your voice for at least a day before your performance. Better yet, think of your speech as an athletic event and go into training—eating right, sleeping well—at least three days ahead.

Be sensible about exercise before your appearance too. It's fine to take a long walk, but don't start training for the marathon the day before you speak. You don't want to stand at the podium and have your muscles screaming at you.

Being tired takes its toll on your nerves as well as on your voice. Being rested will help keep your jitters to a minimum. It's hard to relax when you're tired; you feel as if you'll fall asleep if you let down for a second. And not being able to relax makes nerves that much worse. Decide to be rested.

WHAT TO TAKE TO THE PODIUM

You'll have the text of your speech, of course. If you have typed it out, your sheets should be clipped together, not stapled, so you can slide one page behind the others as you read.

If you're speaking from note cards, make sure they're numbered and securely fastened, with a clip or a rubber band, for your trip to the stage.

Take a handkerchief with you, in case you sneeze or your eyes water or your palms and brow begin to sweat. Tissues shred under this kind of pressure. A cotton or linen handkerchief is best.

Also consider taking a piece of hard candy. Your mouth may get dry, your throat itchy, the muscles in the back of your neck tight. Hard candy will help you avoid the coughing and throat clearing that will tighten you up further. Obviously, you will have to dispose of it discreetly before you speak.

If you can arrange it, drink a cup of hot tea before speaking. And if a glass of water hasn't been provided at the podium, take one (carefully!) along.

Other props are certainly possible. It all depends on what you feel you need. One speaker puts a pocket watch with a large clear face on the podium when she speaks, so she never runs over her time limit—or her audience's lunch break. Another carries a small jar of petroleum jelly and uses it to coat her lips and occasionally her front teeth. She says it keeps her lips from sticking to her teeth when her mouth gets dry with fear. Still another speaker carries a smooth stone in his pocket because it feels cool in his palm, helps keep his hands from sweating, and soothes his nerves.

Take along whatever makes you feel more secure, although showing up at the podium with your teddy bear isn't encouraged. You don't want your audience to know you're *that* scared.

CONTROLLING YOUR NERVOUSNESS

Hiding your nerves, in fact, is one of the best cures for them. Don't fidget as you wait for your turn. You're onstage from the moment you enter the room, and you don't want the audience to catch you in a fit of panic. Sit with your feet on the floor, hands unclenched in your lap. Feel the chair supporting you and breathe deeply, slowly. If your palms are wet, by all means wipe them with your handkerchief.

Talk yourself out of your nervousness or, at least, talk yourself down. Most speakers give themselves mental pep talks while they're waiting to go on. Repeat one of the positive things your practice listeners said, such as "You've got great enthusiasm," or "You have a lovely voice." Or tell yourself something that makes you feel more secure: "I know more about my subject than anyone else here. I'm the expert. I'm here to share my knowledge." You can tell yourself you look marvelous, you're smart, you've worked hard. Make it positive. Make it short. And repeat it, silently, as much as you need.

There are those who suggest you imagine your audience without their clothes on, and say that this is calming. Beware: it might give you a fit of giggles or scare you senseless, depending on who's in the audience.

126

When it's finally time to speak, rise, get hold of your speech, and walk serenely to the podium. No mugging or shuffling, please. Looking calm is half the battle. And self-possession breeds serenity. Whatever jitters you feel, remember that they're natural. Everyone who gets up to speak feels, to a greater or lesser degree, exactly what you're feeling. It's a matter of learning control.

You've been nervous before and lived to tell the tale. And what, after all, is the worst that can happen? Besides, the audience is rooting for you, hoping you'll be wonderful.

Stand calmly at the podium for a moment. Take a deep breath, perhaps a sip of water, then establish eye contact with your audience. Take them in.

After all your rehearsals, you should know the first few sentences of your speech by heart. Glance at your text, look out at the audience, and begin. Remember to speak slowly and clearly. Remember to breathe.

If you're just normally nervous, that's about all it takes. Once you've launched into your topic, your anxiety will subside and you'll begin to enjoy the fruits of your preparation.

But what if you have a worse case of the jitters than you expected? Maybe a lot is riding on your performance, or you didn't get enough sleep, or the competition is fierce.

Don't panic. Instead, get grounded. Nothing is more comforting in moments like these than the awareness that your feet are still touching the floor and the rest of you is still connected to your feet. Feel the floor under you. Breathe. Your breath is your life force, the true energy source: use it. Buy time by taking a sip of water. If your palms and forehead are covered with sweat, say "excuse me" and take a moment to mop yourself with your handkerchief. Remember that the audience can't hear your heart pounding or see your knees shaking. Appear calm even if you can't be calm.

What you are feeling is not so much fear as a form

of excitement. Enjoy the moment, if you can. Relish the edge of nerves; they will give you the power it takes to deliver a really dynamic speech. Hold on to the podium or a nearby table if you must. Establish eye contact with several members of your audience. Remember that they are human beings, not ogres, and that they have come to hear you speak. Don't dance around. Look as poised and confident as possible, glance at your speech, and begin.

While you're speaking, pace yourself. That probably will mean slowing yourself down; nerves tend to make a speaker rattle on very fast. Vary your intonation. Don't rush. Emphasize important points with your voice and gestures. Move around a little; it will help you relax.

Most important, look at your audience. Enjoy what you can. It won't last long. This is your moment: shine!

AFTER YOU'VE FINISHED

Take a moment to acknowledge audience reaction. It will most likely be applause, perhaps wild, perhaps polite. Take it in and relish it. It is one of your rewards for a job well done. Smile at your audience and take your seat. Once you are offstage, don't fidget. Try to remain collected, calm, and poised. If you think you just gave the greatest speech ever, don't gloat. You earned the audience's approval; acknowledge it, enjoy it, and sit down. No raising your arms over your head and clasping your hands triumphantly, please. You'll look more like a chimp than a champ.

If you are less than happy with your performance, don't take out your handkerchief and sob all the way back to your seat. You probably weren't that bad. And if you were, hysterics won't make things better. Maintain your dignity. You can always cry when you get home.

Better than berating yourself, however, is to learn from your experience. What went wrong? How could it

*An enthusiastic, interested audience is the
reward for a well-written, well-delivered speech.*

have been prevented? What would make speaking easier, more fun, more interesting next time?

AND LATER

You'll feel a rush of energy after your speech is finished, a kind of high. It's partly relief that your performance is over. It's partly the pleasure of having been "on." It's a feeling many performers live for. Enjoy it if you can.

Celebrate. Treat yourself to a book you've wanted, a new tape or CD, or a bubble bath.

And, in a day or two, when all the excitement's behind you, take a few minutes to look forward. Imagine with pleasure the next time someone asks, "Say, would you be willing to give a speech?"

CAN I GET A COPY?

Verba volant, scripta manent. ["Spoken words fly
away, written words remain."]

—Ovid

Once you've given your speech, that's the end of it,
right?

Weli, not necessarily. Speeches—especially good
ones—often enjoy a lengthy afterlife. It may be as simple as making copies of your text or notes and distribut-
ing them to those who request them. Or it may be more
complex.

SAY IT AGAIN, SAM

If you did a good job of delivering your speech and
have a compelling message, you could be asked to
speak again. You might be invited to deliver your
speech—or some version of it—to a different audience, on a different occasion.

There's nothing wrong with giving the same speech
more than once. Presidential candidates routinely develop what's called a stump speech, a speech that sets
out their basic beliefs and rouses the crowds to agree
with them. And they deliver that speech over and over,
with minor variations, all along the campaign trail.

While those variations may be minor, they are very
important. Make sure you address your new audience

131

in a way that indicates this speech has been refocused, if not rewritten, with them in mind.

The key is once more to think about your listeners. What makes them different from the group you addressed before? Perhaps you'll be speaking in a different city. Then it might make sense to change any references you made to sports teams, for example, to reflect the local favorites.

You could open with a story about how cold it was the last time you were in Minnesota, or how hot it was when you were in Florida this time last year.

An anecdote that involves hot dogs at Coney Island could become a tale of barbecue in Texas.

You might quote Yogi Berra if you're speaking in St. Louis, but Casey Stengel if you're talking in New York.

Of course, if you can get the names of some of the people who will be in your audience and talk to them about their interests, tailoring your speech to a new group will be simpler.

WORDS INTO PRINT

Sometimes a speech's afterlife takes place in print. One high school principal photocopies his remarks to the graduating class and distributes them along with the diplomas. A business executive mails copies of his successful speeches to people who might be interested in using his company's services.

As long as you've put so much effort into writing and perfecting your thoughts, doesn't it make sense to get more mileage out of them?

Consider who else besides those in your audience might be interested in what you had to say. If your valedictory address accused the school board and the educational system of writing off the needs of students in favor of the bureaucracy, your local paper might print your speech, or an edited version of it.

If you addressed your speech class on the dangers of drinking and driving, perhaps your school paper would be willing to print your views, either as an opinion piece or as a letter to the editor.

If you made your speech on behalf of a group or organization that is seeking contributions or new members, think about mailing your text, or part of it, to your prospects.

If there's a magazine or newsletter that specializes in the subject you addressed, they might be interested in printing some version of your speech. You could turn it into a bylined article or a personal essay. *Writers Market*, an annual publication, lists hundreds of magazines and their specialties. Skim through a copy in the library and see if you can find an appropriate publication for your speech.

Many school districts and newspapers sponsor essay contests on topics like "The Woman Who Is My Role Model," or "How to Promote Interracial Harmony." If your speech is on a related topic, you could rewrite it and enter it as an essay.

If your speech was to a group of prospective students visiting your school, a copy of it could be included in mailings to students who request information about your school.

PERIODICALS THAT PRINT SPEECHES

Extremely good speeches are sometimes reprinted in their entirety. *Vital Speeches of the Day,* published every month, prints "The best thought of the best minds on current national questions." Readers are urged to let the editors know of any speeches that impressed them, so that the editors can obtain copies for review.

Another monthly publication, *The Executive Speaker,* prints the best speeches by business leaders. While your talk may not qualify for inclusion,

you may find some interesting anecdotes, openings, and statistics in the speeches that appear in print.

If sample speeches are what you're after, *Lend Me Your Ears: Great Speeches in History,* edited by William Safire, is a must. In it you'll find models of the very best in oratory from Pericles and Socrates to Boris Yeltsin and Mario Cuomo. The speeches are arranged by type, including memorials and debates, political speeches and farewell speeches, commencement speeches and sermons. While it's unlikely that your speech would be included in the next edition, the collection can give you an idea of what makes a speech great, and how strongly great speeches can affect us.

And, in the end, that is why speeches are important: because they are a way of witnessing events in the world around us. In giving a speech, you have to take a stand. You can affirm your values, denounce the villains, praise the worthy. Speeches are a powerful way of making change happen.

"All epoch-making revolutionary movements have been produced not by the written word, but by the spoken word." That these words were said by Adolf Hitler does not make them false. It merely demonstrates how important it is for those who would change the world for good to speak up effectively, by learning how to give a speech.

The stirring speeches of Winston Churchill, British statesman and master of the English language, are often included in collections of great speeches and are rich sources of memorable quotations.

$\mathscr{F}$OR FURTHER READING

ON WRITING

Barzun, Jacques. *Simple and Direct: A Rhetoric for Writers*. New York: Harper and Row, 1975.

Brande, Dorothea. *Becoming a Writer*. Los Angeles: J. P. Tarcher, 1991.

Goldberg, Natalie. *Writing Down the Bones: Freeing the Writer Within*. Boston: Shambhala Publications, 1986.

Strunk, William Jr., and E. B. White. *The Elements of Style*. New York: Macmillan, 1979.

Ueland, Brenda. *If You Want to Write: A Book about Art, Independence, and Spirit*. St. Paul, Minn.: Greywolf Press, 1987.

FOR QUOTES AND ANECDOTES

Bartlett, John, and Justin Kaplan, general editors. *Bartlett's Familiar Quotations*. 16th ed. Boston: Little, Brown, 1992.

Fadimon, Clifton. *The Little, Brown Book of Anecdotes*. Boston: Little, Brown, 1985.

Fitzhenry, Robert I. *The Barnes & Noble Book of Quotations.* New York: Barnes & Noble, 1981

Kent, Robert W. *Money Talks: The 3,000 Greatest Quotes on Business from Aristotle to DeLorean.* New York: Facts on File, 1985.

Maggio, Rosalie. *The Beacon Book of Quotations by Women.* Boston: Beacon Press, 1992.

Peter, Laurence J. *Peter's Quotations: Ideas for Our Time.* New York: Bantam Books, 1983.

FOR FACTS

Burnam, Tom. *The Dictionary of Misinformation.* New York: Harper and Row, 1975.

Hatch, Jane. *The American Book of Days.* New York: H. W. Wilson, 1978.

Lane, Hana V. *The World Almanac and Book of Facts.* New York: Enterprise Association, revised regularly.

U. S. Department of the Census. *Statistical Abstract of the United States.* Washington, D.C.: U.S. Government Printing Office, annual.

ON CREATING VISUALS

Tufte, Edward R. *Envisioning Information.* Cheshire, Conn.: Graphics Press, 1990.

ON VOICE CONTROL

Peacher, Georgiana. *How to Improve Your Speaking Voice.* New York: Frederick Fell, 1966.

ON HUMOR

Metcalf, Fred. *The Penguin Dictionary of Modern Humorous Quotations.* New York: Viking Press, 1986.

Novak, William, and Moshe Waldoks. *The Big Book of New American Humor: The Best of the Past 25 Years.* New York: HarperCollins, 1990.

Perret, Gene. *Using Humor for Effective Business Speaking.* New York: Sterling Publishing, 1989.

SAMPLES OF EFFECTIVE SPEECHES

Safire, William. *Lend Me Your Ears: Great Speeches in History.* New York: W. W. Norton, 1992.

Wills, Garry. *Lincoln at Gettysburg: The Words That Remade America.* New York: Simon and Schuster, 1992.

PERIODICALS

The Executive Speaker (newsletter). Available from The Executive Speaker, P.O. Box 292437, Dayton, OH, 45429.

Vital Speeches of the Day (monthly). City News Publishing Company, 389 Johnny Dodd Blvd, Suite C, Box 1247, Mount Pleasant, SC 29465. Available at most libraries.

INDEX

ABOUT THE AUTHOR

Margaret Ryan works as a speechwriter for a major corporation. She has also published two books of poetry and is the author of *How to Read and Write Poems*, published by Franklin Watts. Ms. Ryan makes her home in New York City with her husband and daughter.